G. C Bayne

Alphabetical common place book

With References to the Statute Law, and Acts of Parliament, and with

Notes of Cases Decided in the Supreme and Eastern District Courts of the

Cape of Good Hope

G. C Bayne

Alphabetical common place book
*With References to the Statute Law, and Acts of Parliament, and with Notes of
Cases Decided in the Supreme and Eastern District Courts of the Cape of Good Hope*

ISBN/EAN: 9783337084424

Printed in Europe, USA, Canada, Australia, Japan

Cover: Foto ©Suzi / pixelio.de

More available books at **www.hansebooks.com**

ALPHABETICAL
COMMON PLACE BOOK.

WITH REFERENCES TO

THE STATUTE LAW, AND ACTS OF PARLIAMENT,

AND WITH

NOTES OF CASES

DECIDED IN THE

SUPREME AND EASTERN DISTRICT COURTS OF THE CAPE OF GOOD HOPE.

FOR THE USE OF

MAGISTRATES, ATTORNEYS, LAW AGENTS, Etc.

BY

G. C. BAYNE,
RESIDENT MAGISTRATE, BATHURST.

CAPE TOWN: J. C. JUTA.
1885.

LONDON :

PRINTED BY WILLIAM CLOWES AND SONS,
STAMFORD STREET AND CHARING CROSS.

INTRODUCTORY REMARKS.

The Jurisdiction of Resident Magistrates is divided into CRIMINAL and CIVIL.

CRIMINAL JURISDICTION.

The Resident Magistrate is—
1. A Justice of the Peace.
2. A Police Magistrate.
3. A Coroner, and
4. Holds Fire Inquests.

As J. P. it is his duty to enquire, by means of preliminary examination, into all crimes of a serious nature committed within his division, or within two miles of the boundary, or on any vehicle, or railway train passing through such division. The procedure is principally regulated by Ordinance No. 40, 1828, the provisions of which are, with the exception of those sections relating to the duties of a Clerk of the Peace, still in force.

The first step is, generally speaking, the issue of a warrant for the apprehension of the accused, or in some cases, of a search warrant for stolen goods, and an ordinary warrant for the apprehension of the person in whose possession they are found. These warrants are issuable only on sworn information (affidavit q. v.), and a written application for the granting thereof. Such affidavit should be carefully taken down, all hearsay and inadmissible statements being carefully eliminated. It should be precise and regular. The name of the complainant, his residence and occupation should be given, and the circumstances supporting the charge, which should be accurately stated and succinctly made. It will be well if the affidavit winds up with the application "and I therefore request that a warrant may be issued for the apprehension of the said" accused person.

It is noteworthy that the Justice of the Peace before whom the affidavit is made, and he alone, is the proper person to issue the warrant, but such warrant need not command the prisoner to be brought before such J. P., but before any other J. P. or R. M. as may most conveniently meet the ends of Justice. Thus it was held by the judges of the E. D. Court, in a case of defamatory libel, that a magistrate had been wrong in issuing a warrant for the arrest of the accused when the informations had been sworn before a J. P. of the division for the purpose of obtaining the fiat of the Attorney-General, but no warrant issued at the time. A fresh warrant was issued during the course of the preliminary examination by the J. P. presiding, after the examination in chief of the complainant, and this course was, after argument, held correct; the presiding judge remarking that the magistrate had acted correctly in so doing, although he thought it was accidental. Here it may be said that all the preliminaries had been supplied : there were full affidavits made embodying the charge which on the examination in chief were incorporated in the proceedings, the issue of the warrant was applied for by (i.e. directed by the fiat of) the Attorney-General, and the J. P. before whom the information was laid issued the warrant.

In many cases the warrant of apprehension should have a full description of the accused endorsed on it, especially when it is necessary to send such warrant to another magistracy for service. And here it may be well to remark, that as R. M.'s are J. P.'s for the Colony, a warrant issued in their capacity as J. P., will "run" in every district of the Colony, while if signed as R. M. only, it will require to have the concurrence of the R. M. of the district into which it is sent.

The arrest having been made, the prisoner should be placed before the R. M. and then lodged in gaol. Should he then desire to make any statement, he should be cautioned. It is absolutely necessary that the R. M. (J. P.) should caution, a policeman need not do so, though it is advisable that he should. A confession made to a policeman, if voluntary, will be received in Court as evidence, whether the prisoner was cautioned or not, but it is the duty of the R. M. to caution, or the failure will render the confession null and void.

The preliminary examination should take place without unnecessary delay. Every witness should give his full name, address, and occupation, care should be taken especially when the prisoner is undefended, that no evidence is taken down that could not fairly be given, such as evidence of bad character, unless contrary evidence be led, hearsay, statements of contents of documents that may or can be produced, although evidence of previous conviction, should be recorded for the information of the Attorney or Solicitor-General. It is important that the articles stolen, the instrument with which the offence was committed, or any clothing or goods referred to in the evidence, should be carefully labelled in the presence of the witness and the prisoner, and as carefully preserved, while all documents put in as proofs should be consecutively numbered, marginally noted, and attached to the preliminary. In long and important cases, the pages should be numbered and an index made for the use of the prosecution. The manner of conducting the examination is clearly laid down in Ordinance 40, 1828, sect. 31.

It is well to remember that the witnesses should be called in such a manner as to present the facts to the Crown prosecutor in chronological order.

At the close of the examination the prisoner is called upon to state his full name, age, occupation, &c., and is then cautioned and called upon to make any statement he may wish to place on record. And here it may be remarked that the confession of one prisoner will not implicate another prisoner tried on the same charge, or be evidence against him, but merely against himself.

The question of bail next arises, and it is right to remark, that while the prisoner is not, by law, entitled to be admitted to bail during the progress of the case, i.e. from remand to remand, yet it is rarely refused without good reason. At the close of the examination, and on committal, the prisoner is entitled to bail, and the R. M. is bound to fix the amount, and use a judicial discretion in so doing, in all cases except capital offences, or in crimes where some dangerous wound has been given. The bailbond should state some convenient place where the prisoner will accept service of indictment so that the crown may incur no expense.

Should the Sessions or Circuit Court be near at hand, it will be well to enquire of the prisoner whether he will accept "short service" of indictment, &c., and note his acceptance on the record.

The prisoner must be in his "sound and sober senses" (q. v.), or the proceedings will be void.

A case brought under the ordinary jurisdiction, but found to be of too grave a nature for the limited punishment allowed, may be converted into a preliminary examination, but it is not competent to turn a preliminary examination into an ordinary jurisdiction case.

Prisoners should at the close of the examination in chief of each witness called by the Crown, be asked whether they wish to cross-examine, and the statement thus elicited from the witness should also be carefully noted, or the fact that the prisoner declines to cross-question recorded. The doing or omitting of this may affect the admissibility or otherwise of the deposition as evidence at the trial, in the case of the death or illness of the witness.

When taking a prisoner's declaration it is well to draw a fair indictment setting forth all necessary facts (see "Indictment"), dates, places, &c., &c.

As soon as possible after committal for trial a copy of the preliminary examination should be made and sent to the Crown Prosecutor. (Attorney or Solicitor-General or Crown Prosecutor according to position of magistracy.) The prisoner is entitled to obtain a copy on payment of an office fee not exceeding 3d per folio of 100 words. (See "Copy.")

Ordinary jurisdiction of R. M. is given by Act 20 of 1856, as amended by Act 21 of 1876, &c., and by various other Acts referred to in the Index. Under ordinary jurisdiction come such breaches of the law as are called offences as well as petty crimes. Assault, theft, police offences under Act 27 of 1882, the Vagrancy Act, Masters and Servants Acts, Liquor Licensing Act, Ordinance 24 of 1874, and Act 5, 1866-7, Cruelty to Animals Act, Pounds and Trespasses, Ordinance and Municipal Regulations, Burgher Act, &c. &c. (See "Index.")

The prisoner in such cases has been either arrested by the police or brought before the Court on a summons. In many cases a private person can arrest (see " Private Person "), or a summons can be obtained from the Clerk of the Court. In case of the issue of a summons, care should be taken that the person summoned has been allowed his proper number of days notice. (See " Induciæ.")

The printed form of ordinary jurisdiction should always be used, and the indictment carefully drawn. Errors in an indictment can be amended before the prisoner pleads. (See " Indictment.") The offence should be properly set forth. Where *malice, fraud, false pretences, cruelty*, or a guilty knowledge are essential to the crime, the indictment must allege the fact of malice, &c. &c. The case should be headed " The Queen, or Regina, versus ——," occupation and residence of prisoner should be correctly stated, and dates, places, name of person complaining, with occupation and residence. As said of the preliminary examination, the R. M. must satisfy himself that prisoner is in his sound and sober senses, and the evidence should be carefully taken down, as given, as far as possible. This can be done by the R. M. or Clerk, but speaking personally, I have found the best practice has been to take all evidence myself, as fewer inaccuracies occur, and I find it easier to understand the case when I have written the evidence down than if another takes it. I remember a fatal error occurring in an indictment, drawn by a clerk, in a case under the Burgher Act, which I detected and ordered to be amended before the accused pleaded. Through some unfortunate oversight the error remained and the conviction was " quashed."

By some recent decisions of the Superior Courts, it would now seem that perjury is an offence cognizable by Courts of R. M. under ordinary jurisdiction. This will not, of course, extend to any very serious case. Malicious injury to property, when not serious, is also cognizable. But the four crown pleas, rape, robbery, arson, and murder, culpable homicide, assault with intent to do grievous bodily harm (in which some lethal weapon has been employed), concealment of birth, forgery and uttering, serious offences under the Peace Preservation Act, the graver frauds and false pretences, house, store, cellar, breaking with intent to steal and theft, theft of stock in quantities of more than one (and a series of small offences apparently cognizable by Court of R. M., but for which " cumulative sentences " (q. v.) could or would be given in the aggregate exceeding the ordinary jurisdiction), are more proper for the consideration of the Crown Prosecutor. It is better to take a preliminary examination where the nature of the offence is doubtful: or to convert the ordinary jurisdiction case into a preliminary examination should the offence on investigation turn out to be more serious than it at first appeared. Jurisdiction can be given by the remittal of the case. Thus, where some men " broke and entered the house situate at —— of K. M., a labourer, there residing, with intent the goods of the said K. M., there being to steal, and did then and there wrongfully, unlawfully, maliciously and wantonly destroy certain quantity of flour, the property of the said K. M," the case was remitted on a charge of "malicious injury to property." There was plainly no jurisdiction in the R. M. where the house had been broken into, but the case came under the ordinary jurisdiction when remitted.

Although the R. M. sits as a juryman as well as a Judge, he has not precisely the privileges of either. He is entitled, as if a juryman under Act 9 of 1867, to find a prisoner charged of *theft*, guilty of receiving (q. v.) stolen goods, and under Act 21 of 1877, in cases where banker's books are necessary as evidence, the R. M. has the powers of a Judge to grant inspection order, &c. But I know of no other privileges of the sort.

<h3 style="text-align:center">INCREASED JURISDICTION</h3>

is given by Acts 12 of 1860, and 17 of 1867, i. e. under cases remitted by the Crown Prosecutor "plea of guilty," and in cattle thefts where the jurisdiction is extended to one year or 25 lashes for a first conviction, and 36 lashes on second conviction. It should be remembered that the R. M. cannot sentence to imprisonment and lashes under Act 17 of 1867.* He can try a second offence under ordinary jurisdiction, however, when imprisonment for three months and 36 lashes can be given : but the previous conviction must have been had within three years. It is well also to remember that all convictions under the Cattle Thefts Act are to be submitted for review, and that in no case are lashes to be inflicted until the Judge's certificate has been given.

The jurisdiction of magistrates in police offences has been materially increased by Act 27 of 1882, in cases of resistance to police, &c. (q. v.)

<hr>

<h1 style="text-align:center">GENERAL REMARKS.</h1>

It is worthy of note also that in one instance a *furtum usus* (the theft of the use of an article) has been made an offence. (See "Boat.") I refer to Sect. 12, Act 27 of 1882, where the taking a boat without leave is penalized.

By Sect. 31, of Act 20 of 1856, also, the making away with property attached under writ of execution from Court of R. M. is punishable. (See "Embezzlement.")

It is also noteworthy that the punishment of the second offence of drunkenness, by Sect. 9, Act 27 of 1882, is not practically so severe as that provided for the first ; inasmuch as for any second or subsequent offence it is competent to increase the fine, but, according to the Act, neither hard labour nor spare diet can be given.

---

* But see the Act for 1884—not numbered yet or promulgated—G. C. B., July 1884.

Escapes from the gaol or prison itself, are punishable under Ordinance 24 of 1847. Escapes from the precincts of the gaol are punishable under Act 5, 1866–7.

When sentencing females (q. v.) to imprisonment, if hard labour be part of the sentence it is advisable to add " within the precincts of the prison."

Sentence of corporal punishment may properly be recorded as " to receive a whipping, privately in prison, of — lashes." Such additions, as " well laid on, on his bare back," &c., were pronounced improper by Mr. Jacobs, A. G.

Prisoners can be defended, or the prosecution assisted, by any advocate, attorney, or enrolled agent, but it does not appear that any other person can appear to defend or assist the prosecution in criminal cases. (In civil actions this is not the case.)

There is little doubt that a R. M. is justified in fining for theft under the ordinary jurisdiction ; and although by Act 20 of 1856 he is barred from punishing by fine and whipping, yet he is empowered to do so by Act 9 of 1867 (q. v.).

The statute for the summary punishment of juvenile offenders has been practically abrogated by subsequent legislation, by which no corporal punishment is to be inflicted until the certificate of the Judge has been given. The juvenile offender is consequently imprisoned, and in most gaols, exposed to the evil influence of the older criminals, until the record can be sent back to the R. M. The better plan probably is to give the father the chance of chastising the boy in the presence of the chief constable or gaoler.

The Pass Law, Act 22 of 1867, is also practically abrogated by the altered conditions of the colony. Formerly, there were no doubt many " native foreigners " (see "Act "), but of late the natives have in the more settled parts of the colony become peaceable subjects of the Queen, owing no allegiance to any other potentate.

CIVIL JURISDICTION

is that given by Act 20 of 1856, increased by Act 21 of 1876. But it would be impossible within the limits of a short introduction to give any information of practical value. On the question of pleading, which remains in the state in which pleading was thirty years ago, something will be found in the Index, under different headings, " Bailee," " Bar," " Contract," " General Issue," &c.

CUSTOMS LAW.

The Index contains a short alphabetical epitome of the Act 10 of 1872, and of the circulars regulating practice, which it is hoped will be useful.

ALPHABETICAL

COMMON PLACE BOOK.

ABATE has various significations in law. Sometimes imply-
ing—to break down—destroy or remove. Thus, to abate a
nuisance is to put an end to it—to remove it. An action
abates (that is, ceases) by the death of a person (although
not by the death of a trustee in insolvent estate (*vide infra*) :
or is stayed on insolvency pending sequestration.

ABATEMENT. An action against an insolvent estate does
not abate by death of trustee. Ordinance 6, 1843, sect. 54. Stat. Law, p.
567.

———— Pleas of—or in—Nonjoinder of partner, or of husband of
married woman, or guardian of minor (see sect. 51, Act 20,
1856, p. 197, R. of C.). Action pending. Submission to
arbitration. Insolvency of plaintiff or defendant.

ABDUCTION. Crime of. May be committed where female
is of any age under 21 years. Appeal Court, vol. 1,
part 1, p. 37.

———— Exception of want of jurisdiction of R. M. (in civil
suit) upheld. Buchanan, Sup. C. R. 1875, part 2, p. 15.

ABSCONDING insolvent, or insolvent concealing himself,
guilty of fraudulent insolvency. Insolvent Ordinance, sect. 63. Stat. Law, p.
571.

ABSENCE of member of Divisional Council from three consecutive monthly meetings vacates seat (if without leave).
See case of *Searle* v. *Thwaites*, Circuit Court, George. Divi-
sional Council can overlook or condone irregularities. Acts, vol. 4.
Act 4, 1865.
Sect. 58.
p. 155.

———— from Colony with intent to defeat or delay creditors an
act of insolvency. Sect. 4, Ordinance 6, 1843. Stat. Law,
p. 538.

———— of trustee in insolvent estate cause for removal. Sect.
52, Ordinance 6 of 1843. Stat. Law,
p. 566.

———— of defendant in Court of R. M. does not prevent
provisional judgment if service of summons good. Sched.
B. Act 20 of 1856, sect. 28.

ABSENTEE. Joint purchaser. Co-debtor held not liable for
absentee's share of purchase-money of land—unless he were
surety *in solidum* and renouncing all exceptions. Buchanan,
1875, part 4, page 130. Buchanan,
Sup. C. R.
1875.

———— from Colony may surrender estate through authorized
local agent. Ordinance 6, 1843, sect. 2. St. Law, p.536.

B

ABSOLUTION from the instance is a final judgment for the purposes of appeal. Sched. B, Act 20 of 1856, sect. 33.

Buch. S. C. R. 1875, pt. 1, p. 3. ———— from the instance. Witness, if material to defence, to have expenses.

ACCEPTANCE. Verbal acceptance of promissory note is valid : ,but strongest evidence required. 1 Juta 1, p. 33.

Menzies, S. C. R. vol. 1, p. 61. **ACCEPTOR** of promissory note becoming insolvent does not do away with necessity for presentment and notice of dishonour.

ACCESSORY before the fact, is one who directly or indirectly counsels, procures, or commands a person to commit any felony which is committed in consequence of such counselling, procuring, or commandment. 1 Juta 5, p. 399.

ACCOMPLICE giving evidence against partner in crime is thereby discharged from prosecution. 2 Buchanan, part 4, p. 358.

Stat. Law, p. 154. ———— in crime. Competent witness. Sects. 9 and 12, Ordinance 72 of 1830.

———— in crime giving evidence for the *Crown* is secured against prosecution. Sect. 10, Ordinance 72 of 1830.

———— is not compellable to give evidence for private prosecutor unless on certificate of indemnity from Attorney or Solicitor-General or other Crown Prosecutor. Sect. 10. *Ibid.*

———— in crime. His evidence not admissible as testimony against himself. Sect. 11. *Ibid.*

ACCORD and Satisfaction. Something given to or done by defendant for plaintiff, and accepted by plaintiff on a mutual agreement that it shall be a discharge of action. Verbal agreement sufficient. Must co-exist or defence will not be good. (*Pactum de non petendo.*)

ACCOUNTS of Divisional Councils. See section 54, Act 9, 1858; 35, Act 10 of 1864; 85, Act 4 of 1865.

Acts, vol. 5, p. 138. ———— of Divisional Councils to be audited. Act 30, 1875.

Stat. Law. ———— in insolvent estate. Trustee to pay costs if not filed.

Stat. Law, p. 589. ———— in insolvent estate. Trustee to keep for inspection of creditors. Sect. 112, Ordinance 6 of 1843.

Stat. Law, Ord. 40, 1828, sect. 12. **ACQUITTAL** or Conviction of or for any offence, on prosecution by the Crown, no bar to civil action. R. of C. p. 355.

———— A private prosecutor must elect whether he will sue civilly or criminally. Menzies, vol. 1, p. 378.

Stat. Law, sect. 92, p. 584. **ACQUITTANCE** by insolvent, if conclusive, will be null and void.

ACT of Insolvency. Insufficient return to writ of execution is. E. D. R., 2 Buchanan, part 4, p. 245.

ACTION on an account stated. Where there have been dealings between the parties and a balance struck. Defendant may show that any item is not good on account of want of consideration, or that it was stated under a mistake, or was miscalculated under the *plea of general issue*, plaintiff must prove a certain sum to have been admitted. Defendant may prove that account is incorrect, in fact, although he had

Addison on Contracts, 7th edition, pp. 1072 to 1073.

previously admitted it to be correct. Payment or set off must be specially pleaded. Taylor on Evidence.

ACTION against J.P. for anything done by virtue of his office. One month's notice must be given. J.P. may tender amends. Court will consider tender, and if sufficient, J.P. will have costs. Order 32 of 1827, sect. 7. *Stat. Law, p. 97.*

————— on a lease against insolvent estate may be avoided by trustee adopting lease. Ordinance 6, 1843, sect. 104. *Stat. Law, p. 590.*

————— by insolvent for wages, hire, or for labour done, for injury or wrong done to himself or family declared competent. Property purchased by any amount recovered by means of such claim, for injury or wrong done does not vest in or pass under control of trustee. Sect. 49, Ordinance 6, 1843. *Stat. Law, p. 566.*

————— against official in insolvency (Master, R. M. or Commissioner). Official to have same privilege as J.P. Sect.69. *Ibid.* *Stat. Law, p. 575.*

————— against insolvent, if for debt, stayed pending sequestration. Sect. 23. *Ibid.* *Stat. Law, p. 548.*

————— if for breach of contract, stayed until trustee elected. (see *Abate.*)

————— Costs in to be paid by trustee; does not abate by death of trustee. Sect. 53, Ordinance 6 of 1843. *Stat. Law, p. 548, 567.*

ACTS by trustee inferring disqualification. Ordinance 6, 1843. Sect. 42.

————— of Parliament relating to Divisional Councils. Nos. 1 of 1857, 4 of 1865, 21 of 1867, 15 of 1867, 11 of 1877.

————— of Parliament relating to main and divisional roads. Nos. 9 of 1858, 10 of 1864, 22 of 1873, and 11 of 1877.

————— of Parliament. Interpretation or definition of terms. Act 5, 1883.

————— of insolvency defined. Departure from Colony or absence from dwelling house with intent to defeat or delay creditors. Return of *nulla bona* on execution, or not pointing out sufficient property to meet writ, or transferring property so as to defeat or delay creditors. Issue of process of civil imprisonment. Sects. 4, 9, 21, 29, Ordinance 6, 1843. *St. Law, p. 538.*

ADJOURNMENT of meeting in insolvent estate. R. M. or Master may authorize. Ordinance 6 of 1843, sects. 40, 60. *Stat. Law, p. 559. p. 750.*

————— of Court in criminal cases. Witness to attend. Disposal of jury. Act 26 of 1856, sect. 15. *Tennant, R. of C., p. 67.*

————— of Court in civil cases. Penalty for failure. Sect. 15, Act 20 of 1856. *ib., p. 129*

————— in jury trials in civil cases. Sect. 27, Act 7 of 1854. *ib. p. 162.*

ADJUDICATION by Court or malicious or vexatious petition. Insolvent Ordinance 6, 1843, sect. 19. *S. Law, p. 570. p. 549.*

————— of Insolvency may be opposed by creditor. Sect. 17; delayed, sect. 18, or refused. *p. 545.*

ADMINISTRATION of insolvent estate. Ordinance 6, 1843. Sect. 60. *p. 570.*

ADMISSION. An extra judicial admission of a bigamous marriage received in evidence 1875. Sup. Court, R. *Buchanan, p. 99, pt. 3.*

————— of book debts on summons and production of demand. Sufficient in Sup. Courts. Rule of Court 18. *Tennant, R. of C., p. 51.*

B 2

ADVERTISEMENTS of Divisional Council matters. What
Acts, vol. 3, p. 161. to be inserted free in Government Gazette. Sect. 86, Act 4 of 1865.

ADVOCATE or Attorney may practise in Court of R. M. Sects. 40 & 41, Act 20 of 1856. Advocate's fee, 1 guinea. Attorney fee as agent.

Stat. Law, pp. 538, 539. **AFFIDAVIT** of petitioning creditor in insolvency. Sect. 5, Ordinance 6, 1843.

p. 551. —— by creditor or agent as proof of debt. Sect. 27, Ordinance 6 of 1843.

Tennant, R. of C., pp. 93, 137, 138. —— R. M., Master, or J.P. to be Commissioners of Supreme Court for purpose of taking.

AFFIRMATION in lieu of oath by Separatist, Moravian,
ib. p. 427. Quaker, &c. Sect. 7, Ordinance 4, 1846.

AGENCY. Special or general. See judgment by Mr. Justice Smith, *Fame* v. *Lowe*, Juta, Sup. C. R., part 1, vol. 1. p. 18.

AGENT. Power to sell does not as a general principle confer power to receive price, but circumstances may exist from which such power may be implied. 1 Juta 4, p. 289. Voet, 46. 3. 3.

—— Notice of appeal served on: is good, although client has gone away. 1 Juta 1, p. 30.

Buchanan, 1879, S. C. R., part 3, p. 155. —— and principal. Action withdrawn by agent on promise of defendant to pay costs. Agent cannot sue in his own name for costs paid by him.

ib. 1876, S. C. R., part 3, p. 149. —— Enrolled. When suspended or struck off roll. If proceedings have been reviewed and confirmed by judge, the fact will prove a serious obstacle to any re-instatement.

—— Enrolled, fees of. Sect. 38, Act 20, 1856.

—— Enrolled. Fee on admission. Sect. 36, Act 20 of 1856. Admission of.

—— *Ibid.* Proceedings to suspend or strike off roll. Sect. 37.

Buchanan, 1879, p. 170. —— Any person may appear for plaintiff or defendant in civil cases. See *Brown* v. *Hudson*, and R. 13, Sched. B, Act 20 of 1856.

—— Principal may revoke power at any time when no fixed period of service agreed on, unless the agent has an interest coupled with the authority; such as collection of a debt or sale of lands, and payment to agent out of proceeds of debt due to him.

—— is bound to keep proper accounts and vouchers. If goods given to agent to sell, and agent render no account, it will be presumed that goods were sold and money received by the agent.

—— Agents must exercise a reasonable and ordinary amount of care, skill, and judgment. So that if a broker or agent be ordered to buy an article of first-rate quality and he buys a second-rate article, he is liable in an action for breach of contract and damages.

—— An *ordinary* agent is not responsible to his principal for loss caused by the subsequent insolvency of the person to whom he sold if he has acted with ordinary discretion and within his instructions.

AGENT. *Del Credere* agents, by taking higher commissions, render themselves liable to their principals for insolvency of third persons.

AGISTMENT (or depasturing cattle). The duty of an agister is to furnish the cattle under his charge with suitable food, and to give them a proper and reasonable amount of exercise, fresh air, &c. He is bound to take reasonable care of their safety. If he turn them on to a common and they are lost, he is liable. If fence be rotten and bad, he is liable, unless animal got away on account of its own vicious and ungovernable nature and impatience of restraint. *Addison on Contracts, 7th ed., p. 653.*

AGISTOR has no lien upon cattle depastured. 1 Juta 3, p. 185.

AGRICULTURIST. Licensing Act does not refer to sales of wines or spirits by, provided he sell not less than seven gallons at one time, liquors his own produce or distilled by him, but not to be consumed on his own premises. Sect. 2, part 3. Act does not apply to agriculturist selling spirits or wines on public market or to licensed dealer. Sect. 2, part 4. *Act, vol. 6, p. 754.*

ALIBI, Defence of. As proof can be received on indictments that offence was committed on any other day or at any other time not laid in indictment, within three months of the day laid; if defence be alibi, and no particular day be charged, but indictment extended over such period of three months, or a lesser period, so that the accused be prejudiced, R. M. Court will not entertain evidence, and prisoner will be discharged, but will be in the same position as if he had not been called upon to plead (i.e. arraigned). Sect. 14, Act 3 of 1861. *Tennant, R. of C., p. 394.*

ALIENS, Naturalization of. Act 2 of 1883. *Acts, vol. 6, p. 631.*
—— may hold immovable property, but does not acquire right to franchise or office thereby. *Ibid.* *ib.*

ALLEGIANCE, Oath of. Res. Magistrate to take, as well as oath of office. Sect. 6, Act 20 of 1856. Schedule A. *Tennant, R. of C. pp.172,205.*

ALLOWANCE to Insolvent. Ordinance 6, 1843, sect. 59. *St. Law, p.569.*

ALTERATION or Amendment of indictment may be made before prisoner called on to plead. Rule of Court 99. *Tennant, R. of C., p. 82.*
—— in, or deviation from, roads, paths, &c., Governor, and executive may order. Act 11, 1877 sect. 4. *Acts, vol. 5, p. 237.*
—— in promissory note. (Note filled in "Standard Bank") held material and provisional sentence refused. 1 Juta 2, p. 106.

ALTERNATIVE of damages allowed by Supreme Court in suit for specific performance of contract. *Buchanan, 1879, part 4, p. 155.*

AMENDMENT or Alteration of pleadings in R. M. Court. Magistrate may allow if not material or prejudicial, on payment of reasonable costs. Act 20 of 1856, sect. 50.
—— or Alteration of indictment. See "Alteration."

ANIMALS, cruelty to. Act 3, 1875. *Acts, vol. 5, p. 75.*

Acts, vol. 6, p. 251. **ANIMALS** diseased. R. M. to report to Commissioner of Crown Lands. Act 2, 1881, sect. 6.

ib vol. 6, p. 476. ———— slaughtered or left in road. Penalized by Act 27 of 1882, sect. 7, part 8.

ANTE-NUPTIAL Contracts. Invalid unless registered and

Acts, vol. 5, p. 118. a copy filed in Deeds Office. Sect. 2, Act 21, 1875.

ib. Sequestration of estate within two years of date of contract invalidates. *Ibid.* Sect. 3.

Contract invalid against creditors whose debts existed at same date.

Must be notarial. Sect. 9.

Made in any other country must be registered here, and if deposited by notary, whether notarial or not, to have

p. 120. full force and effect as if duly made. Sect. 9.

Payment of premium by insolvent not considered breach of 83rd or 84th section of Insolvent Ordinance.

p. 119. Sect. 6.

Stat. Law, p. 180. **APOTHECARY** and Medical Practitioner. Ordinance 82 of 1830.

Acts, vol. 6, p. 754. ———— Licensing Act does not apply to any liquor sold medicinally by any apothecary, chemist, or druggist, nor to any spirituous or distilled perfume, or perfumery sold by any person. Act 28, 1883, sect. 2, part 1, 2.

APPEAL. As a general rule judgment will not be reversed on a mere question of fact, where there is substantial evidence to support the finding. Appeal Court R., vol. 1, part 1, p. 40; part 2, p. 142.

———— from Court of R. M. Security. Non-prosecution of. Rule 35. Further costs. 1 Juta 3, p. 237.

Vol. 6. ———— Superior Court of. Act 5 of 1879.

———— from decision of R. M. given in all cases. Act 21 of 1876.

Act 20, 1856, sect. 33. ———— in criminal cases (R. M. Court). Rule 33.

———— in civil cases (R. M. Court). Rule 59.

Tennant, R. of C., p. 244. ———— Criminal appeals. Rule 83.

ib. p. 303. ———— Stamp. Act 3 of 1864, sect. 29.

Acts, vol. 5, p. 185. ———— in criminal cases, notice to be given within four days. Act 21 of 1876, sect. 4. (Forty-one days allowed for prosecution of Appeal in Supreme or E. D. Court, and to next ensuing Circuit Court of Appeal made to Circuit Court.)

Tennant, R. of C., pp. 186, 216. ———— in civil cases, notice of appeal to be given to Clerk of Court on next ensuing Court day. Act 20 of 1856, Schedule B, rule 33.

———— Clerk to certify (form given) and transmit record, and to inform parties to suit of session of Circuit Court. Sect. 59.

ib. p. 217. ———— Deposit to be made at time of noting appeal. Rule 60,

p. 218. Sched. B. If appeal withdrawn, within 14 days, deposit to be returned. If not withdrawn applied to opposite party's costs, and surplus, if any, treated as a fine. Rule 35, Sched. B. Act 20, 1856.

Tennant, R. of C., p. 275. ———— Periodical Court within 10 days. R. M. to certify (as in Rule 59 of Act 20 of 1856). Sect. 9, Act 9 of 1857.

APPEAL Sessions of Appeal Court, Cape Town. Buchanan, Sup. C. Rep. 1879, part 4, page 310.

—— allowed by Supreme Court from its own decision in action for £25. Interdict and declaration of right, such right being worth £500. Buchanan, Sup. C. R. 1875, part 3, page 125.

APPLICATION of Divisional Council Funds. Sects. 43, 4, 5, 6, 7, 8, Act 9 of 1858, sect. 11 ; Act 10 of 1864.

APPOINTMENT of R. M. Act 20 of 1856, sect. 5.

—— of Assistant R. M. In cases delegated to him by Governor or R. M. will have same jurisdiction as the R. M. (Cannot issue marriage licence or marry persons.)

APPREHENDED prisoner to be brought before R. M. named in warrant, or if warrant be general, before nearest R. M. with all convenient speed. Ordinance 40, 1828, sect. 32. Tennant R. of C., p. 361.

APPREHENSION, Warrant of. See " Warrant."

ARBITRATION and Award : may be good in part only. This depends upon the deed of submission, and the bad portion must be clearly separable in its nature from the good portion. Buchanan, 1876, part 3. Sup. C. R., p. 37.

ARBITRATOR may administer oaths. Act 4 of 1861, sect. 17. R. of C., p. 434.

ARMS, carrying by night, penalized. Sect. 8, p. 4, Act 27, 1882. Acts, vol. 6, p. 477.

—— carrying or possessing. Unlicensed person within proclaimed districts. Act 13 of 1878. Acts, vol. 5, p. 374.

ARREST of goods as security for rent. Act 20 of 1856, sect. 26. Tennant, R. of C., p. 182.

—— Execution of warrant of. *Ibid.* Sect. 27. p. 183.

—— Inventory of goods attached and notice. Sect. 28. p. 184.

—— If tenant give security, may retain. Sect. 29. See Rule 56, Sched. B. p. 231.

—— Embezzlement or concealment of goods for which such security given is a fraud. Sect. 31. Penalty not exceeding six months. (Warrant for apprehension to issue.) p. 185.

—— Goods so arrested for rent may be sold at once by consent of tenant. Sect. 32. p. 185.

—— and Preliminary Examination. Ordinance 40 of 1828. Tennant, R. of C., p. 357.

—— Who may arrest. See Private Person. Sect. 12, Ordinance 73, 1830 ; also sect. 16. p. 375.

—— Forcible entrance to effect arrest. Sect. 19, Ordinance 73, 1830. p. 378.

—— and release on bail. Ordinance 40, 1828.

—— of criminal. See Buchanan, 1879, part 2. S. C. R., p. 111.

—— of convicts. Sect. 12, Ordinance 7 of 1884.

—— Affidavit to found. Must be clear, distinct, and positive. Rule 8, Rule of Court. Buchanan, Sup. C. R. 1879, part 2, page 41. Tennant, p. 41.

—— without warrant, Act 27, 1882.

—— Accused to be brought before R. M. as soon as possible.

—— Chief Constable may admit to bail in £10, or receive deposit of £10 in offences not serious. Act 27, 1882. Acts, vol. 6.

ARREST. Recognizance recoverable as if taken before J.P. Sect. 19, Act 27, 1882.

Stat. Law, p. 169. —— R. M. Police constable or J.P. may call bystander to assist in. Sect. 13, Ordinance 73, 1830.

St. Law, p. 413. —— Penalty for refusing to assist. Sect. 7, Ordinance 2, 1837.

—— In civil cases, to found jurisdiction and hold to bail, may be issued by R. M. of district for which a Circuit Court

Tennant, p. 101. is to be held. (See Rule 164 and remarks *supra* as to affidavit.)

—— Writ of. Must stand or fall by original affidavit. 1 Juta 3, p. 226.

—— Writ of. Set aside. Not disclosing sufficient grounds for arrest. *Ibid.*

ARSON. Private person may arrest for, if committed in his

p. 376. presence. Sects. 14 & 15, Ordinance 73, 1830.

ARTICLES of the Peace. Irregularities in proceedings. 1 Juta 2, p. 99.

Acts, vol. 2, p. 159. **ART UNION,** legalized lotteries. Act 21, 1860.

ASS. Stallion or entire ass. Trespass by. Sect. 51, Ordinance

Stat. Law, p. 846. 16, 1847.

ASSAULT. An attempt to do a corporal injury to another, coupled with a present ability to do so, or any act or gesture from which an intention to commit a battery may be implied. So, riding after a person and forcing him to run away to avoid being beaten; lifting a stick and threatening to strike another when in striking distance. Battery, which always includes an assault (and the colonial practice seems to be to commingle the two terms in the word assault), is the actual doing of any injury, however small, in an angry, revengeful, or insolent way, such as spitting in a man's face or jostling him. But it is essential that the act done should be against the will of the person assaulted, as a touch or stroke in jest where the parties are only jesting with other, and taking liberties by mutual consent, is no assault. So, touching a friend to engage attention is no assault; but a negligent act is just as actionable as a wilful one, although the intention will be a question for the Court in the matter of damages. Pleas in excuse. Leave and license of plaintiff. Injury done unavoidable, result of superior agency, and conduct of defendant free from fault (sustained). Defence that plaintiff assaulted first and defendant struck in self-defence is good, but defendant must not go too far, or use a lethal weapon in answer to a blow with fist, cane, or whip. Plaintiff may reply excess of defendant. Defence that plaintiff entered defendant's house, and that defendant gently laid hands on him to put him out, good—(*Molliter impositio manus*). This defence is where plaintiff did not enter house with violence, for force may be used to repel force, even without previous request to leave. Where plaintiff is in wrongful possession of land against the will of freeholder, who assaults him in trying to regain possession, the action will not lie. Defence by schoolmaster, or master of apprentice, that assault was moderate and reasonable chastisement. Constables and others acting on warrant may justify. In assault, the private prosecutor must elect whether he will sue civilly or criminally. He cannot have both remedies. Cunningham and Mattinson's ' Precedents in Pleading,' article "Assault," p. 125.

ASSESSMENT of road rates. Sects. 27, 28, 34, 37, Act 9 of 1858; sect. 38, Act 10 of 1864; sects. 7 & 9, Act 5 of 1860.

ASSISTANCE by private person called on by officer of the law. Sect. 13, Ordinance 73, 1830. Penalty for refusing, fine not less than £1 and not exceeding £20, or three months. Sect. 7, Ordinance 2, 1837. *S. L., p. 169.* *ib. p. 413.*

ASSISTANT R. M., Governor may appoint. Act 9 of 1857 (Periodical Court); Act 16 of 1882, sect. 3. If appointed under Act 16 of 1882, to have similar jurisdiction to R. M., but shall be subordinate to him. Sect. 4. May act: 1. When cases delegated by Governor or R. M., and when R. M. is hearing other cases. 2. May be delegated to hold Periodical Court. 3. When R. M. is ill, on leave, or absent on duty.

ATTACHMENT and Inventory. Ordinance 6, 1843, sects. 543, 544.

——— Property pledged by a debtor, and delivered to and left on creditor's property, cannot be attached by messenger at the suit of another creditor who has subsequently obtained judgment. Buchanan, 1879, part 1, p. 49.

ATTESTING Witnesses. Act 22, 1876. Any person may attest wills or other instruments if over fourteen years of age. Cannot witness power of attorney appointing such witness, agent, or attorney. Sect. 2. Legacy left to any person attesting becomes null and void. Sect. 3. Or if person attesting be wife or husband of legatee. Person appointed guardian or executor forfeits appointment by attesting instrument. Sect. 4.

ATTORNEY. Action by. Plea of general issue puts him to the proof that he was employed as an attorney by defendant.

——— Power of, and wills. Ordinance 15, 1845. *S. L., p. 745.*

——— is supposed to be proficient, and is liable to client for damage for want of skill or negligence. Buchanan, Sup. *S. C. R., p. 133.* C. R., 1875, part 4.

——— Articled clerk. Articles must be registered, Rule of Court 213. Buchanan, 1879, vol. 2, p. 73.

——— or Solicitor-General to receive report of all cases under ordinary jurisdiction. Sect. 46, Act 20, 1856; Sect. 13, Act 16, 1864.

———'s Clerk under articles in England for two years, may serve one year in colony and complete. Act 12, 1858; R. of C., 151; Buchanan, 1879, part 2, p. 78.

ATTORNEYS. Admission of. Act 12 of 1858. *Acts, vol. 1, p. 365.*

AUCTION. Sale by sheriff, messenger. Ordinance 92, 1832. *St. Law, p. 225.*

——— sales. Act 5, 1858, dues levied by. 2 per cent. movable, 1 per cent. immovable property. Sect. 1. *Acts, vol. 1, p. 289.*

AUCTION dues and transfer dues. Act 3, 1876.

Acts, vol. 6, p. 754.
AUCTIONEER. Licensing Act does not apply to, if selling for wholesale dealer in such quantities as dealer licensed to sell. Sect. 2, page 6, Act 28, 1883.

——— holding wholesale license may sell liquors by auction. Sect. 16. *Ibid.*

Stat. Law, p. 51.
——— prohibited purchasing at his own sale. Proclamation (probably obsolete).

——— Printed conditions. Parol evidence that auctioneer gave verbal warranty contrary to conditions, held inadmissible. 1 Juta 3, p. 226.

Acts, vol. 5, p. 138.
AUDIT of Public Accounts. Act 30, 1875.

AUDITOR. Divl. Council. Absence of. Election of others. Present at election and acquiescence in, sufficient acceptance. 1 Juta 2, p. 140.

——— Divisional Council, election of. Sects. 79, 80, 83, 84, 85, Act 4, 1865 ; Sects. 4 & 6, Act 15, 1869.

Acts, vol. 4, p. 25.
——— Divisional Council. Office vacated by resignation, insolvency, election as member, becoming contractor with Council, Act 15, 1869.

——— Meeting for election of. Two persons to be duly nominated and seconded. No person to be elected who does not personally accept, or send written acceptance of office to meeting. Failing such acceptance, meeting to proceed to

Acts, vol. 4, p. 24.
election of persons complying with these conditions. Act 15,

ib. p. 25.
1869, sect. 4. Should meeting fall through, or auditor vacate office, C. C. to call fresh meeting at fourteen days' notice. Proceedings as in sect 4. Sect. 6, Act 15, 1869.

Tennant, R. of C., p. 362.
BAIL. Prisoner is not entitled to release on bail. 1st. During course of Preliminary Examination. Sect. 37, Ordinance 40 of 1828. 2nd. When there is doubt as to quality or degree of crime—as, in consequence of a wound and subsequent uncertainty as to death or recovery of person injured.

Murder a capital crime *not* bailable by R. M.

Supreme Court may admit to bail in all cases. Sect. 51, Ordinance 40, 1828.

Prisoner is entitled to bail, if crime not capital, at close of Preliminary Examination. Sect. 46, Ordinance 40, 1828.

Amount of bail to be at the discretion of Judge or Magistrate. No person can be required to give excessive bail. Sect. 53.

R. of C., p. 369.
Expiration of terms of recognizance no bar to trial.

Person discharged from bail not to be recommitted for

Ib.
same offence. Sect. 62.

Person admitted to bail and not brought to trial, not to be liable to find further bail, nor to be recommitted for same offence. Sect. 63.

Addison on Contracts. 7th Edition, pp. 619, 620.
BAILMENT is constituted by the delivery or transfer of any chattel from one person to another, in order that something may be done with it for the benefit of the owner or of the temporary possessor, or for the benefit of both, and the word is applied to the letting and hiring of chattels, as well

as to contracts for delivery of them for safe keeping, or to workmen to be worked upon or dealt with in the course of their employment.

Hirer or bailee is bound to use the article in a reasonable manner, to take the same care of it as he would of his own, and to return it at the time agreed upon, or in reasonable time, in as good condition, as when he received it, subject only to deterioration produced by ordinary wear and tear and reasonable use, or injury caused by accident which happened without fault or neglect of hirer.

If chattels are stolen, hirer must prove ordinary care to prevent. In case of robbery, that it was taken by force. If destroyed by fire that there was no neglect. Hirer of ship not liable for loss by storm except in case of deviation from ordinary course. Whenever through inherent defect some damage occurs, hirer may order necessary repairs at expense of owner.

Gratuitous loan of goods or "mutuum," loan of goods consumed by use and " commodatum " or loan of goods, as a horse or carriage, which are not so consumed. In mutuum hirer must return an equivalent in value or in quantity or quality. In commodatum, the obligation is to return the article itself, subject only to the deterioration resulting from inherent defects or wear and tear and the reasonable use for the purpose for which borrowed. But the borrower is liable for injury or loss if guilty of the least neglect. But he is not liable for inevitable accidents. If a horse is put into his stable by the borrower, and is stolen, he is not liable for the loss, unless he or his servant left the door open. A thing must be used for the purpose for which it is borrowed, or the borrower will be liable even when not in the least neglectful. If horse borrowed for hunting purposes, borrower will not be liable for accident caused by ordinary hunting work. Cunningham and Mattinson's ' Precedents in Pleading,' article " Bailment."

BAKER. Trade. Ordinances 10, 1846, 2, 1838.   S. L., pp. 793,
BANKER. If banker refuse to pay a cheque drawn on him   438.
by a trader who keeps an account with him, and who has sufficient funds in the banker's hands to meet cheque at the time of presentment, the trader can recover substantial damages, as dishonouring a cheque is likely to be very injurious to his credit. No actual damage need be proved.

Different branches of the same company are considered different banks. If, however, balance generally is against customer, cheque drawn on a branch where there are sufficient funds may be refused.

If a banker pay a cheque, erroneously supposing the drawer to have funds, he cannot recover from the person to whom cheque was paid. Cunningham and Mattinson. Article " Bankers."

BANKER'S books as evidence. See " Evidence."

BANKNOTE under £4 prohibited. Penalty £10. Act 6 of 1875. Penalty recoverable in R. M. Court, and leviable under Ordinance 6, 1839.

Acts, vol. 5, p. 80.

—— Duty on. Act 6 of 1864.

p. 81. Vol. 3,

BAR. Prosecution for any crime but murder barred by lapse of 20 years. Ordinance 40 of 1828, sect. 21.

p. 34.

R. of C., p. 357.

—— by prescription. Promissory note and other liquid documents barred after 8 years. Also actions for goods sold and delivered, money lent or advanced by plaintiff for use of defendant, or received by defendant for the use of the plaintiff, including the *conditio indebiti*, rent on leases or contracts, money claimed on account stated—on award of arbitrator, purchase of fixed property, work and labour done, and—or—materials provided, money due on policy of insurance, barred after 8 years. Act 6, 1861, sects. 2 & 3.

Acts, vol. 2, pp. 233, 234.

—— Fees of advocates, attorneys, notaries, conveyancers, land surveyors, medical practitioners (every branch), accounts of bakers, butchers, dressmakers, shoe and bootmakers, tailors, wages of servant, or clerk, barred after three years. (Semble that fees of enrolled agents are not prescribed.)

Except on novation or written acknowledgment to pay —or promise within 3 years, in which case the term is extended to 8 years. Act 6 of 1861, sect. 5.

Acts, vol. 2, p. 234.

BARRISTERS. Admission of. Act 12, 1858.

BEACONS. Land. Acts 7 of 1865, 8 of 1866–7, 11 of 1869, and 9 of 1879.

Vol. 4, p. 18.

BEES. Protection of. Act 9 of 1869.

BEGIN. The right to begin gives right of reply if the other side lead evidence. ' Taylor on Evidence.'

Vol. 6, p. 476.

BETTING. Playing or gambling in street, or open or public place penalized. Act 27 of 1882, sect. 7.

S. C. R., p. 99.

BIGAMOUS Marriage. Extra judicial confession of (letter) received in evidence. Buchanan, 1875, part 3.

Stat. Law, p. 414.

BIGAMY. Person injured by, i.e. illegally married, competent to give evidence, there being no real marriage contract between the parties. Ordinance 72 of 1832, sect. 16.

BILLS of exchange or promissory notes falling due on public holiday or fast or thanksgiving day, payable following day, unless that day be Sunday, when they are payable on the Monday. Act 3, 1856.

Vol. 1, p. 83.

BINDING over to keep the peace. Important case as to issue of summons by one J. P. and decision by another. 1 Juta 2, p. 99.

Stat. Law, p. 743.

BIRTH. Concealment of. Ordinance 10, 1845. R. M. has not jurisdiction except to take preliminary examination.

BIRTHS and Deaths. Voluntary registration. C. C. to keep register. Births must be registered within two months. Cannot be registered after 12 months. Fee to be collected by stamps. (1s.) Act 20, 1880.

Vol. 6.

Vol. 6, p. 478.

BOAT. Removal of, without leave of owner. Statute Theft. Fine £10 or 3 months. Ordinary jurisdiction, Act 27, 1882, sect. 12.

S. C. R., p. 140.

BOND. Breach of condition of. Buchanan, 1876, part 3, p. 140.

BOOKPOST Acts, vol. 2, page 350.

BOOKS, papers and accounts of Divisional Council open to inspection by council, electors, and auditors. Act 4, 1865, sect. 85. *Acts, vol. 3, p. 161.*

BORDER Protection Acts, 27, 1868, 7, 1874.

——— Police Act, 29, 1868.

BOTTLE licence. See " Retail."

BOUNDARIES of Divisions. Ordinance 73, 1830, Act 7, 1873. May be defined or altered by action of both. Divisional Councils Act 33, 1868. *Acts, vol. 4, p. 278.*

BREACH of the peace. Penalty using abusive, &c., language. Act 27, 1882, sect. 10. *Acts, vol. 6, p. 477.*

BREAD. Sale of. Ordinance 2, 1838. *St. Law, p. 438.*

BREED of horses encouraged. Act 15, 1868. *Acts, vol. 3, p. 390.*

BRIBERY at elections. Act 21, 1859, sect. 2 ; Act 9, 1883. Bribery defined as "corrupt practices." *Vol. 2, p. 77 ; vol. 6, p. 672.*

BUCHU. Boekho or Boego plant protected. *St. Law, p. 78.*

BULL. Trespass by. Ordinance 16, 1847, sect. 52. *St. Law, p. 846.*

BUNDLES or parcels. Police may stop persons carrying at night—question and detain. Act 27, 1882, sect. 16. *Acts, vol. 6, p. 479.*

BURGHER and Levies Act 7, 1878. *Vol. 5, p. 339.*

——— Government Office to ascertain exact age of each burgher. 1 Juta 1, p. 55.

——— Cases under Burgher Act to be sent up in ordinary manner for review. 1 Juta 1, p. 64.

——— going on active service cannot be arrested for debt. 1 Juta 2, p. 68.

——— must receive notice to serve. *Ibid.* p. 69.

——— can only be called out in division in which he is resident. 1 Juta 2, p. 73.

——— What is sufficient notice to serve. 1 Juta 2, p. 95.

BURNING grass, stubble, or leaving fire in any open place penalized. Act 27, 1882, sect. 17. *Acts, vol. 6, p. 479.*

BUTCHER'S licence. Any person exposing meat for sale to be deemed to be a butcher for the purpose of requiring a licence. Act 3, 1864, sect. 20. *Acts, vol. 3, p. 300.*

BYE-LAWS. Principles of—i.e. What they must be—lege, fidei, ratione consona. Buchanan, vol. 2, part 4, page 409.

CANCELLATION of adhesive stamps. Power to cancel extended to magistrates and senior clerks to C. C. Act 3, 1864, sect. 14; Act 16, 1876; Act 15, 1877, sect. 7. *p. 179.*

CAPITAL punishment. Act 3, 1869 (does not concern R. M.). *Vol. 4, p. 4.*

CAPTURES in war. Property of a rebel taken vests in Crown. E. D. C. R., 2 Buchanan, part 4, page 272.

CARELESSNESS causing damage to roads. Act 9, 1858, sect. 57.

CARRIER held liable for loss of personal baggage of passenger. 1 Juta 2, p. 125.

——— is a *bailee* when conveying goods.

In action against, for negligence in conveying goods, defendant may prove under general issue that the goods were received by him under an express condition that plaintiff should accompany them for the purpose of protection, and that he neglected to do so; in consequence of which the goods were lost.

In action against. Carrier or other bailee for not delivering or not keeping goods safely, or not returning them on request, the general issue will operate as a denial of any express or implied contract to the effect alleged in the declaration, but not of the breach of such contract. 'Taylor on Evidence.'

Acts, vol. 3, p. 156.   **CASTING** vote. Chairman Divisional Council has not in addition to deliberation vote. Act 4, 1865, s. 63.

CATTLE. Theft of. See "Theft." Act 16, 1864, and Act 17, 1867.

Vol. 4, p. 96.   ——— Removal. Act 14, 1870.

Vol. 3, p. 403.   ——— Licences to depasture. Act 23, 1868.

Vol. 3, p. 398.   ——— Contagious diseases of. Act 20, 1868.

——— theft. Prisoner can be sentenced to pay a fine if shown to have property under sect. 2 of Act 9, 1867, in addition to punishment provided by Act 17, 1867; vol. 2, part 4, Buchanan; E. D. C. R., page 377.

——— thefts. It has been repeatedly pointed out to magistrates that they cannot pass sentence of imprisonment and corporal punishment under Act 17 of 1867. E. D. C. R., 2 Buchanan, part 4, page 384. (But they can take the case as one of theft under ordinary jurisdiction, and for a second conviction the sentence would be a legal one.)

——— Compensation for. Proceedings should be under Act 16, 1861, and not under Masters and Servants Act. E. D. C. R., 2 Buchanan 4, p. 388.

——— Provisions of Sections 43, 47, 48, 49 of Act 20, 1856, extended to all convictions under the Act 17, 1867, sect. 5.

CERTIFICATE for issue of licence. See " Wholesale."

Vol. 3, p. 156.   **CHAIRMAN** Divisional Council. C. C. to be ex officio. Act 4, 1865, sects. 60, 62, 63.

R. of C., p. 397.   **CHARACTER.** Evidence of good. Led by prisoner—lets in previous conviction — formerly charged in indictments as "aggravation." Act 3 of 1861, sect. 19.

Vol. 6, p. 481.   **CHARGE** made under Act 27 of 1882 must be in terms or words of the Act 27, 1882, sect. 23.

S. C. R., p. 152.   ——— Made against prisoner. Prisoner is entitled to copy of summons. Buchanan, 1879, part 3.

S. Law, p. 206.   **CHARTER** of justice.

CHEMIST cannot obtain licence unless holder of certificate

Vol. 5, p. 243.   under Ordinance 82. Act 15, 1877. (Apothecary included.)

CHEQUE drawn to bearer or order is a negotiable instrument without endorsement. E. D. C. R., 2 Buchanan 2, p. 153.

Vol. 5, p. 80.   ——— written in ink. (Good for, &c.) may be for any sum. (This refers to the prohibition of good for, &c., under £3 15s.) Act 6 of 1875.

R. of C., p. 410.   **CHILDREN,** when offered as witnesses to be sworn. Child competent witness if understands nature of oath. Hearsay evidence of statement of child not receivable. Ordinance 72, 1830, sect. 4.

CIRCUIT Court, process to arrest or attach property on action pending, issuable by R. M. of Circuit District. Rule 164. R. of C., p. 110.

CITIZENSHIP. Fingoes to possess in lieu of pass. Act 24, 1857. Vol. 1, p. 270.

CIVIL imprisonment. Plaintiff to pay costs of application for, unless defendant's conduct in non-payment proved to be vexatious. Act 20 of 1856, sect. 22. R. of C., pp. 224, 225.

Rules. Sched. B, 48, 49.

Decree of. pp. 177, 224.

Warrant. pp, 178, 225.

Plaintiff to pay to gaoler costs of detention.

―― imprisonment. Terms offered by defendant. p. 178.

Period of imprisonment: debt £5, one month; over £5 not to exceed three months. Sect. 20. p. 178.

Decree of, will not be granted if defendant prove that he has no means of paying debt. Act 8, 1879, sect. 6. Vol. 6, p. 23.

―― jurisdiction of R. M. Act 20 of 1856, sect. 8; as amended by sect. 2, Act 21 of 1876. R. of C., p. 173.

CLAIMS in insolvent estate, interest on. How ranked and paid. Ordinance 6, 1843, sect. 33. Stat. L., p. 555.

CLERK to R. M. to take down evidence in civil cases, or R. M. may do any act clerk empowered to do. Act 12, 1869. R. of C., p. 279.

―― R. M. Court to take oath of office. Act 20 of 1856, rule 3, Sched. B. ib. p. 206.

―― to C. C., senior, may cancel adhesive stamps. Act 15, 1877, sect. 15. ib. p. 297.

CLUB licence for the sale of wines, &c., does not require certificate of Licensing Board. Act 28, 1883, sect. 10. Acts, vol. 6, p. 756.

―― transfer from steward or manager to successor unnecessary. Sect. 10. ib.

―― licence £18, conveys all "privileges." ib.

COLONIAL produce may be sold without a licence excepting wine and spirits and fermented liquors. Act 11, 1871, sect. 1; Act 10, 1869. R. of C., p. 323, 324.

COMMISSIONER of the Supreme Court for the purpose of taking affidavits and holding to bail. Master, R. M. and J.P. Rules of Court 137 & 138. R. of C., p. 93.

―― civil. Authority under Pounds and Trespass Law. With advice and consent of Divisional Council may establish pounds in each Field Cornetcy. Ordinance 16, 1847, Act 1, 1857, sect. 2; and with said advice and consent may abolish pounds. Act 1, 1857, sect. 4. St. L., p. 827. Vol. 1, p. 207. ib.

COMMITTAL for trial. If R. M. find sufficient grounds, he shall grant warrant clearly expressing crime or offence. Ordinance 40 of 1828, sect. 35. p. 362.

―― must precede trial, but prisoner may be tried for another crime than that for which committed by R. M.

―― will be presumed unless defendant shall prove the contrary. Act 15, 1864, sect. 5. Vol. 3, p. 402.

COMMON assault. Jury may find persons accused of rape, murder, &c., guilty of. Act 15, 1864, sect. 3. Acts, vol. 3, p. 401.

COMPULSORY sequestration. See " Sequestration," " Undischarged Insolvent," " Preferent."

Stat. Law, p. 539.

Creditor to the amount of £50, or two creditors whose debts jointly amount to £100 may petition for. Act 6, 1843, sect. 6.

CONCEALMENT of birth. See " Birth."

—— of property to defeat attachment in insolvent

S. L., p. 554. estate.

CONDITION precedent. General issue does not put in issue the performance of a *Condition precedent*, whenever the consideration of the promise is executory. For instance, where the consideration for the defendant's promise was that the plaintiff would assign certain shares and pay certain money, and the declaration contained an averment that the plaintiff did assign the shares and pay the money, the averment was held not to be denied by the general issue. Also where the consideration was the delivery of 20 tons best lead, and the averment that the lead was delivered, defendant was not allowed to show, under the general issue, that the lead was of inferior quality.

CONFESSION of prisoner. R. M. *must* caution before taking; must be voluntary, and is evidence against person

S. L., p. 418. making. Ordinance 72, 1830, sect. 28.

p. 419. —— by A is not evidence against B. *Ibid.* Sect. 31.

—— of prisoner. Buchanan, E. D. Court, vol. 1, part 1, p. 26.

—— to constable admissible if voluntary. Buchanan, 1876, part 2, p. 57.

p. 562. **CONFIRMATION** of election of trustee in insolvent estate by Supreme Court.

p. 572. **CONSEQUENCE** of not lodging inventory, or of refusing to be examined.

pp. 572-3. —— to third parties of refusal to be examined.

CONSIDERATION, as well as the promise. General issue plea does not put in issue one and the other. Defendant can prove any material variance between the consideration for his promise and that proved by the written agreement. He may disprove the consideration, because by the plea of general issue he denies the contract.

CONSTABLES, gaolers, turnkeys, &c., to give month's notice

Vol. 5, p. 146. of resignation. Act 1, 1876, sect. 1.

—— chief, shall execute criminal process in all districts

p. 403. where there is no sheriff. Act 15, 1864, sect. 6.

yp. 302-3. **CONSTRUCTION** of roads. Act 22, 1873, sess. 5, 6, vol. 4;

Vol. 3, p. 43. Act 10, 1864, sect. 2.

CONTEMPT of Court of R. M. Prisoner undergoing trial cannot be punished by R. M. for. See also Act 20, 1856, sect. 54.

—— of R. M. Court. An agent re-possessing himself of money paid into Court as a tender, and refusing to give it up again, commits a contempt. Proceedings against agent, if certified by judge, a serious difficulty in the way of hearing subsequent application. Buchanan, 1876, part 3, p. 149.

S.L., p. 544. **CONTINGENT** creditor. How to prove and rank claim. Ordinance 6, 1843.

CONTRACT of service, made out of Colony, must be certified by Consul or other proper officer, or by magistrate of place. Act 15, 1856. For *oral* or verbal contracts see vol. 1, Acts; sect. 2, Act 15, 1856. Acts, vol. 1, p. 108. p. 109.

—— Defence to action for *goods sold* that they were sold under a special contract that they should be shipped during the current month and landed at London within a certain time, which conditions were not performed, is admissible under general issue. p. 250.

Work and labour done. Under the general issue it may be shown that the work was so negligently and unskilfully done as to be valueless; or that part of the work was done and material supplied by the defendant. Amount of work done and material supplied is not a set off but a deduction. p. 250.

Money lent and paid. Defendant may show, under *general issue*, that there was an agreement that plaintiff should lend him money or pay money for him in consideration of his endorsing a bill, or depositing with him bonds and other securities, with a power to sell and reimburse himself, which conditions were performed by defendant. p. 251.

Letting and hiring. (*Locatio-conductio.*) Defendant may show, under *general issue*, that he never rendered himself liable, in point of fact, to payment of rent; or that the premises were uninhabitable; or that there has been no actual entry by him; or that his occupation was not by sufferance of the plaintiff; or that he occupied premises by permission of prior owner, to whom he has paid all arrears of rent without notice of assignment to plaintiff; or that he was let into possession by plaintiff under a contract to purchase, which contained no stipulation as to the terms of occupancy, and fell through because plaintiff could not make out a good title. In action on every species of contract, all matters of confession or avoidance, including not only those by way of discharge, but those which show the transaction to be void or voidable in point of law, on the ground of fraud or otherwise, shall be *specially pleaded:* e.g. infancy, coverture, release, payment, performance, illegality of consideration either by statute or common law, drawing, endorsing, accepting, &c., bills or notes by way of accommodation, set off, mutual credit, unseaworthiness, misrepresentation, deviation and various other defences. Lunacy, intoxication, material alterations, should also be specially pleaded; but partnership with plaintiff, and that claim is from the unsettled partnership account, or that the instrument sued on is not stamped, or insufficiently stamped, may be raised under the general issue. p. 254.

In simple contracts, as for example, actions for goods sold, work and labour done, money lent, paid, received, or found due on account stated, property sold, rent, hire of goods, freight, &c., the general issue operates as a denial of those matters of fact from which the defendant's liability arises. In action for goods sold and delivered, the plea will

c

operate as a denial of the bargain and sale, or sale and delivery, in point of fact; for money had and received as a denial both of the receipt of the money and of the existence of those facts which make such receipt by defendant a receipt to the use of the plaintiff. Defendant may show under this plea, in action for goods sold, that he paid ready money, that they were sold on a credit not yet expired, when the action commenced, that they were bought through an agent and the price remitted to that agent before the expiration of the credit, or that they were sold under a condition that they should answer a certain purpose or nothing should be paid for them: that they were sold under a special agreement which has not been performed: that they did not answer the description of articles plaintiff professed to sell: or that they turned out perfectly useless. Defendant may prove in reduction of damages under general issue: that goods supplied were of less value than prescribed by the contract. If action brought for goods sold and delivered, and the contract prove to have been for the supply of material to be used by the plaintiff in the construction of a building or other fixture for defendant, defendant will succeed under general issue, for in such case the plaintiff should sue for wood, labour and materials, or for erecting and constructing the building.

Special Pleas are *necessary* as follows: Under general issue defendant cannot show that goods did not belong to the vendor, or that he was not entitled to them at the time; and that the real owner reclaimed them. When goods had been sold, which were liable to forfeiture, and actually were seized and condemned by the Revenue officers after delivery to purchaser, in action for the price it was held that defendant was right in *pleading* specially, admitting an actual sale and delivery, but excusing non-payment on the ground of the seizure and consequent failure of consideration. *Ibid.*

Acts, vol. 1, p. 247.

CONTRACT of service. Insertion of penal clause does not do away with general right of dismissing from service, or of cancelling contract. Buchanan, 1876, part 2. S. C. R., p. 74.

—— Declaration may contain an alternative count for work and labour done.

—— Privity of. Mere receipt of money by one person for another to be paid to a third person does not give such third person a right to bring action against such receiver. Buchanan, 1879, part 1, p. 16.

Vol. 1, p. 109.
ib.

—— before R. M. can only be made for five years, and if extra Colonial can also last five years only. Act 15, 1856, sect. 5.

—— form of.

—— by old Divisional Council binding on new Act 4, 1865, sect. 76.

—— Ante-nuptial. Act 21, 1874.

R. of C., p. 404.
p. 397.

CONVICTION, previous, how proved. Act 7, 1867.

—— Notice to be given. Act 3, 1861, sect. 20.

p. 395.

—— previous, or acquittal for that offence, prisoner stating fact sufficient plea. Act 3 of 1861.

CONVICTION of witness for crime does not render him incompetent to give evidence. Ordinance 14, 1846, sect. 2. *R. of C., p. 425.*
———— quashed. Prisoner cannot again be tried for same offence. 1 Juta 2, p. 90.
———— R. M. cannot pass another sentence. 1 Juta 4, p. 308.
———— previous. Sect. 24, Act 3 of 1861, does not apply to Court of R. M. No notice is necessary. 2 Juta 1, p. 2.
CONVICTS. Ordinance 7, 1844; 10, 1844; 1 of 1845. Act 5, 1866; Act 1, 1876.
COPY of document, account or bill, usually attached to summons. If Court consider defendant was not prejudiced by omission to serve, case need not be dismissed on this account. Act 20, 1856, rule 10. *p. 209.*
———— of preliminary examination. Prisoner committed for trial is entitled to, on payment of 3d. per folio of 100 words, within reasonable time. Sect. 11, Act 17, 1874. *p. 408.*
———— Prisoner at trial may inspect depositions without fee. *Ibid.* Sect. 12. *ib.*
COPYRIGHT. Foreign reprints of: pay 20 per cent. duty *ad valorem.* Books to be stamped. Act 4, 1854.
———— Act. Protection of authors. Act 2, 1873. *Acts, vol. 4, p. 247.*
COSTS in cases where plaintiff and defendant reside in different divisions, or action against officer of R. M. Court, will be judged of by Superior Court as if action could not be brought otherwise. Act 20, 1856, sect. 35.
———— of action brought in Superior Court that might have been entered in Court of R. M. Judgment obtained for amount that Court of R. M. could have given, only R. M. Court costs will be given. Act 20, 1856, sect. 34. *R. of C., p. 187.*
———— If judgment for defendant, he will have costs as between attorney and client. *ib.*
———— of appeal not prosecuted, refused. 1 Juta 3, p. 237.
———— Discretion of R. M. in, must be exercised judicially. R. M. refusing costs on account of antiquity. Held that he had not acted judicially and judgment reversed. 1 Juta 4, p. 285. Buchanan, 1879, page 4. *p. 232.*
CREDIBILITY of a witness. It is competent to support or impeach, according to English Law. Ordinance 72, 1830, sect. 48. *p. 423.*
CREDITOR petitioning for compulsory sequestration.
———— Amount of debt. Ordinance 6, 1843. *St. Law, p. 539.*
———— may accompany messenger making inventory. *pp. 543–4.*
———— conitngent: proof and ranking. *p. 554.*
———— may have special meeting called to prove his debt, at his own expense. *p. 568.*
———— proving debt may vote. *p. 559.*
CRIMES committed within Colony are all under the jurisdiction of the Supreme Court. Ordinance 40, 1828, sect. 1; or of Circuit Court for district. *Ibid.*; or of inferior Court established by Governor. *Ibid.* Sect. 3. *p. 352.* *p. 353.*
CRIMINAL jurisdiction of R. M. under Act 20 of 1856, sect. 42. Ordinary.
———— procedure where no Clerk of the Peace. Ordinance 8, 1852.

Vol. 4, p. 61–4.
Vol. 5, p. 380.
CROWN lands. Disposal of, regulated. Acts 4, 1870; 5, 1870; 14, 1878.

S. C. R., p. 169. ——— property not liable to municipal taxation. Buchanan, 1879, part 3.

Acts, vol. 5, p. 75. **CRUELTY** to animals. Act 3 of 1875. "Wantonly or cruelly beating or ill-treating, overdriving or abusing, wounding or torturing, or causing any of the above acts to be done" to any domestic animal.

——— to animals. The words "wantonly or cruelly" are words of substance in indictment under Act. 2
pp. 102, 390. Buchanan 1, E. D. C. R., 2 Buchanan 4.

R. of C., p.376. **CULPABLE** homicide: private person may arrest for. Ordinance 73, 1830, sects. 14, 15.

Stat. Law, p. 576. ——— insolvency: act constituting. (Crime within jurisdiction of R. M.) Ordinance 6, 1843, sect. 71.

CUMULATIVE sentences by magistrate, whereby the prisoner may have to undergo a term of imprisonment exceeding in the whole the jurisdiction of the R. M., should be avoided. It would be better to take a preliminary examination for a series of charges. In any case it is well to remember that a succession of convictions had at the same does not act as "previous conviction within two years," i.e. a thief is convicted of a crime on the 14th, and of a similar crime on the 30th; the theft of the 14th will not act as a previous conviction to that of the 30th, if sentence pronounced same day.

CUSTOMS Law. (See Appendix.) Act 10 of 1872, &c., alphabetically epitomized.

——— officer selling wine, spirits, &c. Act 28, 1883, does not apply to. Sect. 2, sub-sect. 5.

DAMAGE done to roads by carelessness. Act 9, 1858, sects. 46, 47.

Stat. Law, p. 549. **DAMAGES.** Property acquired by means of damages recovered by action for injury done to insolvent or family does not come under sequestration. Ordinance 6, 1843, sect. 24.

DANGEROUS wound given. Private person may arrest if
Stat. Law, p. 356. crime committed in his presence. Ordinance 73, 1830, sects. 14, 15.

Stat. Law, pp. 262, 263. **DEATH** notice: nearest relative to send in to R. M. Form of. Inventory of goods (page 266).

ib. ——— of trustee in insolvent estate. Proceedings to elect a
p. 566. new trustee. Judge's order. Ordinance 6, 1843, sect. 52.

Stat. Law, p. 549. **DEBT** of creditors petitioning for compulsory sequestration. Necessary amount. Ordinance 6, 1843.

p. 558. ——— within what period may be proved. *Ibid.* Sect. 37.

ib. ——— proved after payment of a dividend does not disturb that dividend. *Ibid.*

——— of public bodies. Act 11, 1867.

R. of C., p. 176. ——— Court may order payment of, by instalments. Act 20, 1856, sect. 11.

DECLARATION substituted for extra-judicial affidavit. Ordinance 6, 1845.

DECLARATION of dying person made under apprehension of death, admissible or not according to English Law. Ordinance 72, 1830, sect. 43. Stat. Law, p. 422.

DEEDS. Mode of stamping. Act 17, 1873.

DEFAMATION OR DEFAMATORY LIBEL. Anything written or printed and then published that is given to the world not necessarily in print, which is false and must tend to injure the reputation of another, or expose him to hatred, contempt, or ridicule, is a libel and actionable as such without proof that the plaintiff has actually suffered pecuniary loss or injury of any kind from the act of defendant. It is not, therefore, essential to set forth the actual damage, although it is usual, when any special damage has been sustained, to increase damages.

—— Distinction between *Libel* and *Slander.* ("Injuria literalis ") and ("Injuria verbalis.")

It is not law to say that anything *spoken* which is calculated to injure the reputation, &c., is actionable, unless the plaintiff has actually sustained damage. But spoken defamation that: 1st. Plaintiff committed any indictable offence. 2nd. That he has contracted a contagious disease, unfitting him for general society. 3rd. An imputation affecting his profession or trade, or imputing incompetency, dishonesty, or disgraceful and improper conduct in relation thereto, *are actionable, per se.*

Truth of a libel is an answer in a civil court. In criminal cases this defence will not avail, unless the publisher show it was for the public good.

Malice is an important averment. If defendant can rebut imputation of malice, his liability is at an end.

Publication is material. The libel *must* be published, or given to the world, but if any person besides the defamer and defamed has seen it, that is sufficient publication. A letter containing a libel, and misdirected, is published as soon as read, and from that moment plaintiff has a ground of action.

The plaintiff must be identified with the libel. The libellous matter must be set out verbatim. If in a foreign language, it must be averred, that the person who read it understood that language, or there would be no publication.

Defences. That the words written or spoken were true in fact is a good defence if it can be proved strictly and precisely. But it is a dangerous plea. 1st. In a case recently decided, it was held that defendant was not justified in calling the plaintiff a "felon," although he had been convicted of felony, if he had undergone his sentence. 2nd. If not proved, it is regarded as express malice.

Privilege must be specially pleaded. Defendant acted bonâ fide, and published the words complained of on a justifiable occasion.

Absolute privilege. Words spoken by a Member of Parliament, in Parliament, by Judge during action, by counsel, evidence of witness, report by military man to superior officer, and evidence on courts martial.

Qualified privilege. Fair report of judicial proceedings. Meeting of a board. Statement by members of a municipality to meeting of councillors held privileged, &c.

That defendant did not publish.

That the words have not the libellous or defamatory meaning imputed.

That they do not apply to plaintiff.

Accord and Satisfaction (q. v.) form a good defence if duly pleaded and substantiated.

Mutual apologies agreed to.

See Defamatory Libel Act and title " Libel " h. l.

Newspaper proprietor may plead that words were published without actual malice or gross negligence, and that an apology was made by first opportunity and a sum of money paid into Court as amends. Cunningham and Mattinson's ' Precedents in Pleading.' pp. 281 to 286.

DEFAMATORY Libel to have same meaning as in England by law existing in 1882. Act 46, 1882, sect. 12.

DEFENCE of Criminal by advocate, attorney or agent. R. of C., p. 193. Act 20, 1856, sect. 45.

DEFENDANT, non-appearance of, in criminal cases, when bail has been found. Bail bonds may be estreated and R. of C., p. 74. warrant of apprehension granted. Rule of Court 75.

ib. —— on non appearance of prosecutor may move the Court to p. 75. discharge him. Rule of Court 76.

—— in civil cases, Court of R. M., may appear by any person he authorizes in writing. If person not advocate, attorney or enrolled agent nothing allowed, in taxation, for his services.

—— absent, power may be signed for him by any one having pp. 209, 210. general authority to manage his affairs. Act 20, 1856. Sched. B., Rule 13.

Acts, vol. 6, p. 754. **DEFINITION** of intoxicating liquors, under Act 28, 1883, i.e. Liquors that require a licence. Sect. 3.

ib. —— of terms of Act, 28, 1883, sect. 3.

DEPOSITIONS to be taken in writing and on oath. Ordin- S. Law, p. 360. ance 40, 1828, sect. 31.

DERELICT lands. (See " Quit Rent.") Act 3, 1879.

Acts, vol. 4, p. 55. **DESERTERS** from army. Apprehension of. R. M. to investigate circumstances and make return. Act 1, 1870.

DESTITUTE children. Apprenticeship of. Person with whom child is left to bring to R. M., or give notice to Field Cornet. Penalty for detaining child not more than 20s., and not less than 5s. for each month allowed to elapse without Acts, vol. 1, p. notice. Act 15, 1856, sect. 6. Child shall be taken to R.M., 114. who shall make enquiries as to relatives, give notice in *Gazette,* and apprentice to some fit and proper person should no relative apply.

Vol. 5, p. 237. **DEVIATION** of roads, paths, &c. Governor may authorize. Act 11, 1877, sect. 41.

DISQUALIFICATION for wine and spirit licence. Act 28, 1883, sect. 8. — Vol. 6, p. 756.

DISTRICTS for election of members Divisional Council. Act 4, 1865, sects. 3, 4, 5. — Acts, vol. 3, p. 138.

DIVIDEND on debts not due: in insolvency. Ordinance 6, 1843, sect. 29. — S. Law, p. 553.

DIVISION for Council purposes to mean fiscal, not electoral. Act 4, 1865, sect. 78.

DIVISIONAL and main roads vested in Council. Act 10, 1864, sect. 2. — Vol. 3, p. 43.

—— Police Force. Act 8, 1873. — Vol. 4, p. 258.

—— Boundaries. Both Councils can represent necessity for alteration of. Act 33, 1868. — Vol. 3, p. 427.

—— Council cases. R. M. who is ex officio chairman cannot sit. Buchanan 1875, part 2. — S. C. R., p. 78.

—— Council with C.C. to establish, and abolish pounds in division. Act 1, 1857, sects. 2, 4. — Vol. 1, p. 207.

—— Councils. Acts specially affecting, 4, 1865; 15, 1869.

—— Boundaries. Two Divisional Councils to agree upon, and submit proposed new boundaries. Governor may by proclamation declare such new boundaries. Act 33, 1868. — Vol. 3, p. 427.

DOCUMENTARY evidence, and other articles produced and put in as evidence in criminal cases, to be labelled or marked in presence of persons so producing. Ordinance, 40, 1828, sect. 41. — S. Law, p. 363.

DOG. Setting dog on any person, or allowing dog to worry any person or animal. Act 27, 1882, sect. 8, sub-sect. 9. — Vol. 6, p. 476.

DOGS. Doing damage in vineyard or enclosed garden where grapes grow, between 1st December and 1st April in any year may be destroyed. Ordinance 16, 1847, sect. 50. — S. Law, p. 846.

—— Injury to property by. See " Scienter."

DOG TAX. It is not ultra vires for Municipality to impose. Buchanan 1875, part 3, p. 101.

DOMESTIC servant, not specially engaged for longer period, to be considered monthly servants. Act 15, 1856, sect. 2. — Vol. 1, p. 109.

DOMESTICATED Ostrich. See " Ostrich." Act 4, 1868. — Vol. 3, p. 330.

DOUBT, in seduction, to be given in favour of the defendant. Buchanan 1875, part 31. — S. C. R., p. 120.

DRIVER of any vehicle, misconduct of. Keeping wrong side of road, parts 1 & 3. Being away from his cattle, part 2 (or guard), using abusive language, or by intoxication, endangering persons, or demanding more than proper fare, part 5. Act 27, 1882, sect. 7. — Vol. 6, p. 476.

DRUNKENNESS, &c., in public place penalized. Act 27, 1882, sect. 9. — p. 477.

DUCES TECUM, Subpœna. Act 20, 1856, Rule 17, Sched. B. — R. of C., p. 211.

DUES. Transfer. Ordinance 13, 1844. Acts 15, 1855; 7, 1868 ; 3, 1876.

EJECTMENT. Action of. Jurisdiction of R. M. in. Act 20, 1856. Tennant's Rules of Court. — R. of C., pp. 175, 180.

Warrant to put in possession. Sect. 24. — p. 181.

Warrant not to operate as satisfaction for rent. Sect. 51. — p. 227.

R. of C.
p. 182.

When there is no movable property, Court may decree delivery up of possession. Sect. 25.

EJECTMENT *Lease. Sub-letting.* Ejectment for breach of condition not to sub-let decreed. Sub-letting, if a breach of contract, is sufficient to sustain action for. Buchanan, 1875,

p. 8.

part 1.

ELECTED for more wards than one. Member of Divisional Council to notify which ward he will represent. Act 4,

Vol. 3, p. 155.

1865, sect. 48.

ELECTION of members of Divisional Council, Act 4, 1865.

——— to be triennial and on second Wednesday in October in

Vol. 3, p. 155.

1885, 1888, 1891, &c. *Ibid.* Sect. 57.

——— Registration of voters, qualification, &c. Act 14,

Vol. 5, p. 14.

1874.

——— of trustee in insolvent estate at second meeting. Or-

S. Law, p. 549.

dinance 6, 1843, sect. 25.

——— of trustee. If one candidate has a majority of votes, and another a majority of value, there is no election.

ENDORSEMENT by R. M. or J.P. for any other district : or by Field Cornet of the particular Field Cornetcy in which person to be summoned resides, must be served by person

R. of C., p. 189.

authorized to serve. Act 20, 1856, sect. 52.

——— of writ of execution by R. M. of another district. *Ibid.* Sect. 13, page 176.

ENROLLED agent. See " Agent."

ENTICEMENT. There must be absolute enticement of men from their work to enable employer to prove that he has been

p. 32.

wronged. 1 Juta 1.

Evidence of, proves that wrong was committed, which entitles plaintiff to recover even when not proving special

p. 276.

damage. 1 Juta 4.

ESCAPE of prisoner from lock up under special J.P. Magistrate to have jurisdiction as if he had escaped from gaol, i.e. under Ordinance 24, 1847. Act 5, 1866-7.

——— of prisoner from gaol, refers to precincts of gaol. Act 5, 1866-7.

EVIDENCE. Rules of. 1st. Evidence must correspond with the allegation, but the substance only of the issues may or need be proved. 2nd. Evidence must be confined to the points at issue. 3rd. The *onus probandi* is on the party holding the substantial affirmative. 4th. The best evidence, of which the case, in its nature, is susceptible, must always be produced.

——— Parol : to vary written conditions of sale not admissible. 1 Juta 3, pp. 229, 232.

——— of accomplice. If given at request of public prose-

p. 358.

cutor discharges accomplice. E. D. C. R., 2 Buch. 4.

R. of C., p. 413.

——— of accomplice. Court may commit on unsupported testimony of : if crime proved to have been committed. Ordinance 72, 1830, sect. 12.

——— Confession, if voluntary, is : against person making it.

p. 417.

Ibid. Sect. 28.

EVIDENCE, Law of. Follows English Law.
—— Banker's books to be admitted as : on affidavit by officer Acts, vol. 5, p. of bank. Act 21, 1877. 252.
—— or duly certified copies of. *Ibid.* Sect. 2. Ten days' notice to produce necessary. Sect. 3. Bank cannot be compelled to produce ledgers, &c., except on judge's order. Sect. 4. Unless bank is party to action. R. M. may give inspection order. Legal proceedings to mean civil or criminal suits. R. M. has power as a judge. Sect. 8. But proceedings must be pending.
—— to be taken in writing in civil cases.
—— Objection to evidence or any document to be noted. Act 20, 1856, sect. 24. R. of C., p. 214.
—— Prisoners' confession made to constable admissible as: if voluntary. Buchanan, 1876, part 2. S. C. R., p. 57.
EXAMINATION of insolvent before R. M. on oath. Ordinance 6 of 1843, sect. 61. S. L., p. 570.
—— Special, of insolvent. *Ibid.* Sect. 62. p. 571.
—— If insolvent does not show good cause for absence, and does not attend, warrant may issue. Insolvent cannot refuse to answer any questions. *Ibid.* Sect. 64. p. 572.
EXCEPTION to set off pleaded to claim by plaintiff. Amount of set off due as executor allowed. Buchanan, 1875, part 3. S. C. R., p. 126.
—— to jurisdiction of R. M. in civil suit for abduction upheld. Buchanan, 1875, part 4.
—— to jurisdiction of R. M. in Divisional Council case. Buchanan, 1875, part 2.
—— of want of consideration. Buchanan, 1876, part 3, p. 131.
EXECUTION of judgment. Act 20 of 1856, sect. 12. Wearing apparel, bedding and tools, to value of £5 excluded. *Ibid.* Sect. 15.
EXECUTORS, trustees, tutors, or curators, to lodge accounts with master within twelve months, or may be summoned by Acts, vol. 3, p. master. Act 14, 1864, sect. 1. 70.
—— will lodge wills, codicils, &c., with R. M., who will compare and authenticate copy with his signature. Act 11, 1873, sect. 5. Copy to be registered, Act 11, 1873, sect. 6, and will have force of original if original lost. *Ibid.* Sect. 7.
EXPENSES of third parties, required as witnesses in insolvencies to be tendered them. Ordinance 6, 1843, sect. 66. S. Law, p. 573.
EXPROPRIATION of land for main roads, toll houses, &c. Act 9, 1858, sect. 10 ; Act 10, 1864, sect. 3.
—— of land for divisional roads. Act 9, 1858, sects. 46, 47.
EXTRADITION of criminals. Offences committed in Free State or Transvaal. Acts 19 of 1872 ; 17 of 1877 ; 22 of 1882.
FAILURE to nominate a candidate as member for Divisional Acts, vol. 3, p. Council. Act 4, 1865, sects. 54, 55, 56. 152.
—— to elect a member of Divisional Council. *Ibid.* Sect. 53.
FALSE Imprisonment. A total restraint of the liberty of the person for however short a time, " even by forcibly detaining the party in the streets against his will, will amount in law

to an imprisonment, and if such imprisonment is unjustifiable it will amount to a false imprisonment and be actionable. An arrest or imprisonment, however, is not confined to a corporal seizure." If a person send for a constable, and give another in charge for felony, and the constable tell the person charged that he must go with him, and he, in order to prevent the necessity of actual force being used, expresses his readiness to go, and does actually go, this is an imprisonment. (Abbott, C. J. in *Pocock* v. *Morse*, Ry. & Mo. 321.) But although there need not be an actual seizure of his person to constitute imprisonment, the restraint on his liberty must be total. A partial restraint, as by preventing a person advancing along a particular pathway, while allowing him to retire, is not enough. (*Bird* v. *Jones*, 7 Q. B. 742–752.)

Defences.—1st. Defendant justifies, on the ground that he was executing legal process. 2nd. Where defendant cannot plead that he was actually executing a warrant, but can set up that he had reasonable and probable cause for believing the plaintiff had committed an offence for which he was by law justified in arresting him.

Arrest under warrant.—Constables, bailiffs, sheriffs, executing are protected, although the warrant be irregular.

J.P. issuing warrant.—If J.P. have no jurisdiction he is liable to an action; but if he have jurisdiction plaintiff can only recover on showing that he acted maliciously and without reasonable and probable cause.

J.P. entitled to notice.—By English and Colonial statutes, any J.P. must have one month's notice of action. Plaintiff must show that conviction was quashed, and J.P. can tender amends. By Ordinance 32 of 1827 these actions against J.P. are barred after six months. See 'Addison on Torts,' chap. 15, sect. 3.

See also *"Private person arresting."*

R. of C., p. 190.   **FEES** of enrolled agents. Act 20, 1856, sect. 38.

ib.   ———— of enrolled agents allowed in taxation.

ib.   ———— of costs of successful suitor. Sect. 39.

———— in liquid cases, 7*s.* 6*d.* ; in illiquid, 10*s.* Sect. 39.

———— Court has discretionary power. Sect. 39.

———— of office and fines to be paid to Clerk of Court.

Vol. 5, p. 246.   ———— collected by means of stamps. Act 16, 1877, sects. 1 & 2.

Stat. Law, p. 829.   ———— of Poundmaster under. Ordinance 16, 1847, sect. 7.

All subject to alteration by Divisional Council Act.

FEMALE Debtors. Magistrate cannot refuse decree of civil imprisonment for, on the ground of there being no accommo-

S. C. R., p. 85.   dation for females in the gaol. Buchanan, 1875, part 2.

R. of C., p. 192.   **FEMALES** not liable to corporal punishment or to hard labour in streets, &c. Sect. 43. (Sentence of female should always have the proviso attached, " within the precincts of the gaol," if hard labour form part of sentence.)

FERÆ NATURÆ, not necessary to prove " Scienter " in

S. C. R., p. 51.   case of damage by such animals. Buchanan, 1876, part 1, p. 51.

FEROCIOUS animal. Owner is always liable for injury done by, as he is bound to keep it securely.

FERRIES and gates of toll-bars. Property of Divisional Councils. Act 10, 1864, sect. 4. *Acts, vol. 3, p. 43.*

FIELD Cornets and Assistants, appointment of. Ordinance 5, 1837. See 'Manual for Field Cornets.'

FINES and penalties under Stamp Acts, 3, 1864, and 13, 1870, may be recovered by criminal process if not over £50. In uncertain cases in Superior Courts. In case of procedure in Court of R. M., the person aggrieved may appeal on paying penalty and giving security to the satisfaction of R. M. for costs. Act 13, 1870, sect. 10. *R. of C., p. 328.*

———— and penalties for offences not exceeding £40 may be recovered in R. M. Court, unless express provision made ; and in case of non-payment, distress may be levied on goods of offender. Ordinance 6, 1839. *Stat. Law, p. 461.*

———— and penalties, recovery of. Offender, if committed, to be released on payment of fine. Informer to receive not exceeding one-half and not less than one quarter of. *Stat. Law, p. 462.* *p. 463.*

FIRE made in any open place, or applied to stubble, grass, or trees, penalized. Act 27, 1882, sect. 17.

———— Inquests' Act. R. M. to hold proceedings. Costs. Person may be apprehended. R. M. to report to Attorney or Solicitor-General. Deposit. Witnesses' expenses. Decision to be given in open Court. *Vol. 6, pp. 792, 793.*

FIREARMS and gunpowder. Ordinance 2, 1853 ; Act 11, 1875 ; Act 29, 1879. *Vol. 5, p. 89.* *Vol. 6, p. 71.*

FORCIBLE entrance into house to arrest criminal. Every law officer and every private person acting under 14th and 15th sect. of Ordinance 73, 1830, may make. *R. of C., pp. 376, 377, 378.*

FOREST and Herbage Preservation Act, 1859. Contravention by "Juvenile Offender," punishable by (not exceeding 25) lashes or cuts with cane or rod. Act 19, 1877, sect. 2. *Vol. 2, p. 73.*

———— or mine land, not to be treated as waste crown land. Act 14, 1877, sect. 15. *Vol. 5, p. 384.*

FORGERY. Crime of uttering, &c., indictment for. See "Indictment."

FORMÂ pauperis, action in. Mechanic in receipt of good wages cannot sue. Buchanan, 1876, part 1. *S. C. R., p. 9.*

FORMS of plaint. Act 20 of 1856. In R. M. Court summons according to such form held good. *1 Juta 3, p. 177.*

FRAUD, defence of, is available when there has been some concealment or deception practised by the plaintiff with regard to the transaction in question. Where a fraudulent representation constitutes the alleged fraud, it must be as to a matter which, in the case of a simple contract was substantially the consideration for the agreement. If plaintiff represents such and such a state of affairs to exist, knowing nothing about them, and such a state of affairs does not exist, such reckless statement is a fraudulent representation and will vitiate the agreement. Hiring a house for a person stated to be respectable, and such person turning out not to be respectable, is a good reason for refusing possession. Fraud may consist in intentionally allowing a person to remain under a mistake affecting his estimate of the value of a property. Mere concealment of a defect will not amount to fraud where person is under no obligation to disclose it. Knowingly permitting a person to remain under a misrepresentation made by a stranger will vitiate a contract. Fraud on the part of an agent will vitiate a contract as a rule. Cunningham and Mattinson, ' Precedents in Pleading,' article " Fraud."

Acts, vol. 3, p. 55. FRAUDULENT marking of goods. Act 12, 1864.

—— Insolvency. Insolvent absconding, or concealing himself so as to evade examination, guilty of. Ordinance 6,

S. Law, p. 571. 1843, sect. 63.

p. 575. —— Insolvency, what acts constitute. *Ibid.* Sect. 70.

p. 599. —— Insolvent, not entitled to discharge. *Ibid.* Sect. 118.

p. 604. FRESH surrender by undischarged insolvent. *Ibid.* Sect. 128.

FRIENDS or legal adviser of prisoner cannot have access to prisoner *before committal* except on authority of R. M. *After committal* may have free access, subject to regulations of R. M.

p. 362. Ordinance 40, 1828, sect. 38.

FUNERAL expenses are a preferent claim. Trustee cannot be sued, if creditor has filed his claim, before filing account of liquidation. Buchanan, 1876, part 1. S. C. R., p. 50.

FURNITURE, household, of insolvent. Sold on resolution of

S. Law, p. 587. creditors. Ordinance 6, 1843, sect. 98.

—— How it can be retained. *Ibid.* Sect. 99.

GAME Law. 2nd March, 1822.

GAMING, playing, betting in street or open place penalized.

Vol. 6, p. 476. Act 27, 1882, sect. 7, part 13.

—— or gambling. Any licensed person suffering any unlawful game or gambling to be carried on, penalized. £10. Act 28, 1883, sect. 73, part 4.

p. 769. —— debts cannot be recovered by action at law. Buchanan, 1875, part 1. S. C. R., p. 4.

Vol. 5, p. 146. GAOLER, absence of. Act 1, 1876.

—— to receive civil debtor on warrant. Act 20, 1856, sect. 18.

—— Plaintiff to pay charges for maintenance of debtor, or gaoler may release. Charge 1s. per diem, weekly in advance.

R. of C., p. 178. *Ibid.* Sect. 18.

—— indemnified for releasing rehabilitated insolvent.

GAOLERS to send in list of persons confined within their respective gaols to Registrar of Circuit Court, and to Registrars of Supreme and E. D. Courts if within jurisdiction. Criminal

R. of C., p. 367. Sessions. Ordinance 40, 1828, sect. 56.

GAOLS. Ordinance 24, 1847 ; Act 1, 1876.

GATES. Owner or occupier of land may erect swing gates

Vol. 5, p. 238. across roads, paths, &c., on his property. Act 11, 1877, sect. 5 ; Act 37, 1879.

—— Penalty for improperly opening, or not properly closing same. Sects. 1 and 2, Act 37, 1879.

GAZETTE. See " Government."

GENERAL Issue. Plea still used on Circuit and in Courts of R. M. Some information will be found under headings "Contract," "Agent," "Bailee," &c.
—— issue and plea of tender cannot be made together to cause of action. Buchanan, 1875, part 2. S. C. R., p. 38.
—— and plea of tender following. Does not remove liability for costs. *Ibid.*
—— plaintiff objecting to plea of tender as bad and insuffi- S. C. R., p. 40.
cient pleaded after general issue cannot compel defendant to abide by tender. *Ibid.* p. 49.
—— title to land in trespass cannot be proved under. *Ibid.* 1876, part 1. p. 7.
—— in action for right of way, effect of. *Ibid.* 1876, part 2. p. 65.
GENERAL Law Amendment. Act 8, 1879, Lœsio enormis abolished. Sect. 8.
—— decree of civil imprisonment cannot be granted if defendant has nothing. Sect. 6.
General law in mercantile matters made English. Does not alter law of pleading or notarial practice. Sects. 1, 2, 4.
—— abolition of law providing that contracts of lease shall become void or voidable, or rent irrecoverable through non-productiveness of ground on account of inundation, tempest, or unavoidable misfortune, or that lessor himself has absolute need of the land leased. Sect. 17.
GLANDERS. Ordinance 5, 1844; Act 7, 1866-7. Provisions Acts, vol. 3, p. of Act extend operation of ordinance to mules and asses. 253.
GLASS. Wilfully breaking any pane of glass. Act 27, 1882, sect. 7, part 10.
GOODS sold and not delivered. Risk still attaches to seller. (*Periculum rei venditæ.*) Buchanan, 1879, part 2. S. C. R., p. 91.
GOVERNMENT Gazette. Notices concerning Divisional Councils to be inserted free of charge. Act 4, 1865.
Notice to nominate member. Sect. 16.
Notice to candidate unopposed and elected. Sect. 25.
Notice to members elected. Sect. 45.
Notice calling first meeting. Sect. 46.
Notice of failure to elect. Sect. 52.
Notice of failure to elect. Sect. 53.
—— Gazette. Insolvent estate. Trustee to notify seques-tration and his appointment in or removal by Master. Ordi-nance 6, 1843, sect. 55. S. Law, p. 567.
—— Gazette. Production of, as proof of proclamation of district under Peace Preservation Act, 13 of 1878, and of establishment of Reformatory Act, 7, 1879.
GOVERNOR'S sanction necessary to cancellation of stamp after 62 days. Act 5, 1864, sect. 15.
GRAND and Petit Juries. Ordinance 84 and Act 7, 1861.
GRANTS to Divisional Council from Government. Act 22, Acts, vol. 4, p. 1873, sect. 3. 301.
GRAVEL to repair roads. Council may take from quit rent lands. Buchanan, 1876, part 2. S. C. R., p. 105.

Vol. 6.	**GUN**, pistol, or other weapon, carrying at night. Act 27, 1882, sect. 8, part 4.
	Without permit in proclaimed districts. Act 13, 1878.
Acts, vol. 3, p. 114.	**GUNPOWDER**, dealing in, regulated. Ordinance 2, 1853. See Act 28, 1864.
ib. p. 114.	Offences under ordinance to be charged as contravening ordinance as amended by Act 14 of 1857, and made perpetual by Act 28 of 1864.
ib. 267.	Permit for. J. P. not being dealer in, may grant. Act 14, 1866–7, sect. 2.
Vol. 5, p. 89.	——— Form of permit. See Ordinance 2 of 1853. ——— Law Amended Act 11, 1875. Penalties to be construed as if the words " not exceeding " were inserted before the amounts of fines and terms of imprisonment. Sect. 2.
ib. 240.	——— and Firearms Act 13, 1877. Governor may prohibit issue of ammunition, sect. 2, including cartridges, sect. 5.
	——— Natives cannot acquire firearms, &c., without permission of Governor or Secretary Native Affairs. Sect. 4. (But see Act 13, 1878, sect. 5.)
	——— Permits. Governor may authorize clerk to R. M. to issue. Act 29, 1879.
	——— Register of permits to be kept and copy sent, *certified correct*, to Colonial Secretary in January and July. Act 29, 1879, sect. 3.
S. Law, p. 352.	——— Private magazines. Ordinance 7, 1834.
p. 354.	——— Regulations for landing. Ordinance 7, 1834.
	HABEAS Corpus. Buchanan, 1879, part 2. S. C. R., p. 45.
Acts, vol. 5, p. 188-9.	**HARBOUR** Board may make regulations for order, to be approved by governor. Fines or imprisonment not to exceed ordinary jurisdiction of R. M. Act 2, 1877.
ib. vol. 3, p. 250.	**HARD** labour, prisoner working outside gaol. Discipline Act 5, 1866–7. See "Prisoner."
	——— in streets, or corporal punishment. Females cannot be sentenced to either. Act 20, 1856, sect. 43.
R. of C., p. 323.	**HAWKER**, who shall be deemed. No person selling fish, fruit, vegetables, milk, eggs, butter, poultry, wild fowl (not being game), cakes, confectionery, honey, flowers, brooms, charcoal, horsebedding, lime, mats, baskets, straw hats of colonial make, or firewood, Act 10, 1869, sect. 1 ; or any article (except wine, spirits, or fermented liquors) being colonial produce. Act 11, 1871, sect. 1.
ib. p. 324.	——— not liable in damages for selling goods on public road running through land the property of a shopkeeper. Buchanan, 1879, part 2. S. C. R., p. 74.
Acts, vol. 6, p. 640.	**HEALTH** Act (Public). Act 4, 1883.
	HEARSAY evidence inadmissible when it would not be received in Courts of Record at Westminster. Ordinance 72, 1830, sect. 44.
S. Law, p. 422.	
ib. 356.	**HEIRS**. Wife or next of kin may prosecute for death of person. Ordinance 40, 1828, sect. 18.

HERBAGE and Forests Protection. Act 18, 1859.   Vol. 2, p. 73.
HOTELS, Canteens, &c., for sale of liquors. Properly authorized person may enter upon ground supposing liquor unlawfully sold. Refusal to admit, or delay in admitting penalized.
Act 27, 1882, sect. 14.   Vol. 6, p. 478.
────── or any other house on similar grounds. Same penalties for refusal or delay. *Ibid.* Sect. 15.   ib. p. 479.
HOURS for sale of liquors without privileges defined by part 2, sect. 7 of Act 28 of 1883.   Vol. 6, p. 755.
HOUSE DUTY. Act 20 of 1878.   Vol. 5, p. 395.
HUSBAND may prosecute for injury done to wife. Ordinance 40, 1828, sect. 16 (see also sect. 15).   R. of C., p. 356.
────── (or wife) competent witness against and may prosecute the other in case of injury done by either. Ordinance 72, 1830, sect. 15.   S. Law, p. 156.
────── and wife. Promissory note signed by both. Buchanan, 1876, part 2, p. 55.
────── and wife. Payment to wife of money by her brought into community on husband's absence or possible death. Buchanan, 1876, part 3. S. C. R., p. 130.
HYPOTHECATED Goods. See "Pledged" and Buchanan, 1876, part 1.   p. 17.
IDLE and disorderly persons, definition of. Act 23, 1879, sects. 2, 3, 4, 5, 6.
ILLEGAL or immoral consideration. No action can be brought on a promise to do an illegal act, nor can an action be brought on a promise made for an illegal consideration, or for a consideration consisting of several parts, any one of which is illegal.
────── Printer cannot recover charges of printing a libellous or blasphemous work.
────── Money lent for the purpose of playing an illegal game cannot be recovered, but money paid by an agent at the implied request of the principal in fulfilment of a wagering contract, may be recovered from such principal.
────── Bond to secure payment of a racing debt is void.
────── Letting or hiring for immoral or illegal purposes cannot be recovered if person had knowledge of the purpose.
────── Bond given in consideration of future illicit co-habitation is illegal, for past is legal.
────── Illegality or immorality must be specially pleaded, and facts on which defence is founded must be stated.
ILLIQUID document. A written order requiring oral evidence before plaintiff could recover is not a liquid document. 1 Menz. 62. 1 Juta 1, p. 35.
ILLNESS of member of Divisional Council, notice of, to be given to Council. Act 4, 1865, sect. 58.   Acts, vol. 3, p. 155.
IMMEMORIAL time. Defined as period of proscription. Buchanan, 1876, part 2. S. C. R., p. 65.
IMPLEMENTS of housebreaking, possession of, without lawful excuse. Act 27, 1882, sect. 8.

INCEST. Carnal intercourse between persons connected by affinity is punishable as. Buchanan, 1875, part 3. S.C.R., p. 98.

INDECENT exposure through insufficient clothing punishable under Act 23, 1879, sect. 8, part 1.

INDICTMENT may be amended before prisoner has been called upon to plead. Rule 99. *(R. of C., p. 82.)*

———— Definition of, by Act 3, 1861, includes any charge or complaint in Court of R. M., and any plea, replication, or pleading. Act 3, 1861, sect. 30. *(Acts, vol. 2, p. 400.)*

———— in describing joint stock company or firm : may be described under style or title; not necessary to mention individuals. Act 15, 1864, sect. 2. *(R. of C., p. 401.)*

———— for *Murder.* Sufficient to charge that accused did wrongfully, unlawfully, and maliciously kill and murder deceased. Act 3, 1861, sect. 4. *(ib. pp. 390,391.)*

———— Misjoinder of crimes. E. D. C. R., 2 Buch. 4. *(p. 401.)*

———— *Culpable Homicide.* Sufficient to state that accused did wrongfully and unlawfully kill the deceased. Act 3, 1861, sect. 4. *(pp. 390, 391.)*

———— for *Forgery, Uttering, &c.* Sufficient to describe the instrument by name by which usually known. No copy or facsimile necessary. *Ibid.* Sects. 5 & 6. *(p. 391.)*

———— for *Fraud.* Sufficient to allege *intent to defraud* without stating intent to defraud any particular person. *Ibid.* Sect. 7.

———— The words "intent to defraud" are not absolutely material. It is sufficient to allege that accused did "falsely and fraudulently" make certain representations. Appeal Court, vol. 1, part 1. *(p. 19.)*

INDORSER of promissory note. Law provides safeguards for, one is presentation of bill on due date. S. C. R., 2 Juta 1. *(p. 15.)*

———— Provisional sentence against refused, the maker having been released. Buchanan, 1876, part 3. S. C. R., p. 158.

INDUCEMENT is that portion of the declaration or summons which contains a statement of the facts out of which the charge arises, or which are necessary or useful to render the charge intelligible.

INDUCIÆ. (Service of indictment.) In reckoning ten days, day of trial must be excluded. Service of summons and distance. Rules regarding. Supreme Court, Rule 2. *(R. of C., p. 125.)*

———— Summons in Court of R. M. Rule 10, Act 20, 1856. Shortest distance forty-eight hours. *(ib. p. 209.)*

INFANT. Child under seven years of age cannot be convicted of crime. Van der Linden, p. 288. E. D. C. R., 2 Buch. 4. *(p. 392.)*

INFANTICIDE. Prisoners found guilty of concealment of birth. Conviction quashed on ground of irregularity. Sect. 24, Act 5, 1879. Appeal Court, vol. 1, part 1. *(Vol. 6, p. 10. p. 22.)*

INFANTS are only liable on contracts for necessaries. Matters of mere ornament are not generally necessaries, unless they are for an infant of high station. Necessaries for infant's wife are on the same footing as if supplied to infant himself (see Roscoe V. 635–6). Promissory note drawn during infancy. Infant is liable as soon as he attains majority. Warranty. Infant not liable. But if "emancipated," working for himself, and not domiciled with father is personally liable.

INHERITANCE of minors. Widower or widow to pay minor's share to master or pass deed of "kinder bewys." Act 12, 1856.

―――― Magistrate to certify (on receiving certificate that law has been obeyed in this respect, or affidavit that there was no property in the estate) that "it has been made to appear that no reason exists arising out of unsecured inheritance of minor children, why the banns of marriage of widower (or widow) should not be published." *Ibid.*

―――― Amended law. Act 26, 1873.

INQUESTS provided for. Act 22, 1875. Magistrate to hold if within six miles of residency, otherwise the Field Cornet. Witnesses allowed expenses as at criminal trials or preliminary examinations. Acts, vol. 5, p. 121.

INSANE persons. Safe custody of dangerously insane. Act 20, 1879.

―――― person purposing suicide or intending to commit indictable offence may be brought before R. M., who may, on certificate of two medical men, send lunatic to hospital. Sect. 1.

―――― Governor may release or send back to prison. Sect. 2.

INSOLVENCY. Collusive agreement not to oppose rehabilitation. Penalty, forfeiture of claim. E. D. C. R. 2 Buch. 2. p. 109.

―――― Meetings called. No creditor appeared. No trustee elected. Insolvent held entitled to discharge. 1 Juta 1, p. 49.

―――― or assignment of estate by member of Divisional Council vacates seat. Act 4 of 1865, sect. 58. Vol. 3, p. 155.

―――― of Auditor. Act 15, 1869, sect. 5.

―――― how constituted. Ordinance 6, 1843. S. Law, p. 538.

―――― Election of trustee in. See "Election."

INSOLVENT on obtaining order to file list of creditors with Master. Inventory to be made. Cannot acquire property during insolvency. Sect. 49. p. 543. p. 564.

―――― cannot bind, cede, transfer, or convey, except as an agent. Can work for hire, and sue for and recover wages, free from control of trustee. See also Act 15, 1859. p. 565.

INSPECTION of roads and bridges by Government. Act 22, 1873, sect. 2. Vol. 4, p. 301.

―――― of goods delivered, to ascertain exact quantity, plaintiff to have. Buchanan, 1875, part 3. p. 96.

―――― of documents in libel case refused. 1879, part 4. p. 204.

INSTALMENTS. Court may order payment of debt by, whether plaintiff consent or not. Act 20, 1856, sect. 11. R. of C., p. 176.

―――― Failure to pay instalment. Execution may then issue. Act 20, 1856, sect. 14. p. 177.

INSUFFICIENTLY clothed persons may be dealt with under vagrancy. Act 23, 1879, sect. 10. Vol. 6.

INSURANCE, law of, to be English. Act 8, 1879.

D

INTERDICT to abate nuisance. Competent for any one of public to apply for. Buchanan, 1879, part 1, p. 2.

S. Law, p. 425.   **INTEREST** in action does not render witness incompetent to give evidence. Ordinance 14, 1846, sect. 3.

———— accrues from date of demand; and if no demand, from date of service of summons. Buchanan, 1875, part 3, p. 93.

———— Judgment given for interest reserved by bond, although notice of increase had been given. *Ibid.* 1876, part 3, p. 157.

INTERIM allowance to insolvent. Ordinance 6, 1843, sect. 59.

S. Law, p. 569.
ib.   ———— care of estate may be given to insolvent.

Vol. 6, pp. 659 to 661.   **INTERPRETATION** of terms in Acts of Parliament. Act 5, 1883.

INTERPLEADER action, in case of claim made by third persons to goods attached by messenger. Act 20, 1856, sect. 53 and Rule 58.

INTERROGATORIES to be sent to witness resident in another district may be given, to be forwarded by R. M.

pp. 197, 198.   "on Service." Act 20, 1856, sect. 52.

INVENTION. Patents for. Act 17, 1860.

INVENTORY of goods attached for rent to be furnished to tenant. Sect. 28, and notice Rule 55, Act 20, 1856.

———— in insolvent estate if not lodged. Ordinance 6, 1843,

S. Law, p. 572.   sect. 64.

IRREGULARITIES for which proceedings may be set aside.

R. of C., p. 353.   See "Review."

IRREGULARITY in proceedings. On an application for exhibition of "Articles of the Peace," the J.P. who ordered security to be given was proper person to commit for default. 1 Juta 2, p. 99.

Vol. 5, p. 206.   **IRRIGATION** promoted in the colony. Act 8, 1877.

Vol. 6, p. 69.   ———— by municipalities assisted. Act 28, 1879.

JOINT Stock Companies, winding up Act. Act 12, 1868.

Vol. 3, p. 338.   Limited Liability Act. Act 23, 1861.

JUDGE in vacation, power of. Act 23, 1875. One judge has

Vol. 5, p. 126.   all the power of full bench. *Ibid.* Sect. 1.

JUDGMENT of, and sentences by, magistrate to be given in

R. of C., p. 214.   open Court and recorded by clerk. Act 20, 1856, Rule 26.

———— against insolvent stayed pending sequestration. Or-

S. Law, p. 547.   dinance 6, 1843.

R. of C., pp. 186, 187.   ———— of R. M., how appealed from. See "Appeal" also.

JURISDICTION of R. M. in civil cases exercisable over or in respect of any person residing in or inhabiting district

R. of C., p. 173.   assigned to. Act 20 of 1856, sect. 8. Sched. B, Rule 1.

———— in criminal cases in respect of any offence committed within boundary, or within two miles of boundary of district, or in respect of any property in a cart, &c., having passed

R. of C., pp. 191, 192.   within two miles of such boundary. See also "Railway." Act 20, 1850, sects. 42 and 44.

———— in liquid cases, increased to £100 (not on mortgage bonds however). Defendant may object, and have case re-

Vol. 5, p. 185.   moved to a Superior Court if over £40. Act 21, 1876.

JURISDICTION. Appeal given in all cases decided by magistrates. *Ibid.* Sect. 3. Notice in writing within four days.

JURORS, Qualification of. Ordinance 84, 1831. Acts 7, 1861; and 2, 1876.   R. of C., p. 435.

JURY in civil cases. Acts 7, 1854; and 30, 1874, trial by, in civil cases. New trial. Buchanan, 1879, part 3.   p. 156.

JUS in re. Delivery is necessary to pass dominium. Buchanan, 1876, part 3.   p. 115.

JUSTICES of the Peace created. Ordinance 32, 1827.

———— Special. Act 10, 1876.

JUVENILE offenders, Act 21, 1869. Cuts with the cane (lashes), corporal punishment of any sort cannot be inflicted until proceedings have the approval of a judge. Acts 21, 1876; and 19, 1877.

KAFIR Emissaries. Punishment of. Act 26, 1857.

KILLING peace officer when in execution of his office defined as murder. Ordinance 73, 1830.   R. of C., p. 377.

KOURÈ Railway Act, No. 5, 1881.   Vol. 6, p. 255.

KOURI Harbour. Improvement company dissolved. Vol. 4. page 25, Act 16, 1869. Wharfage and cranage dues at. Vol. 3, page 257, Act 3, 1866-67; Ordinance 4, 1852 amended, schedule of dues substituted. *Ibid.* Sect. 1. Persons landing goods to declare value to officers of customs. *Ibid.* Sect. 2. Declaration as per Schedule 2. Officers may take bond for payment of wharfage. *Ibid.* Untrue declaration equivalent to perjury. *Ibid.* Sect. 3. Dues on wool, 6d. per 100 lb. landed or shipped. Schedule 1. All other goods, 10s. per £100 value ($\frac{1}{2}$ per cent.). *Exemptions.*—1st. Public stores, naval, military and personal baggage. 2nd. Ships' stores. 3rd. Goods on which dues paid on importation. 4th. Coastwise goods. 5th. Bullion. Vol. 5, page 10, Act 11 of 1874.

LAMP or lamp-post, injury to. Act 27, 1882, sect. 7, part 2.

LAND Beacon's Act. Appointment of commissioners to take evidence. Buchanan, 1879, part 3.   p. 148.

———— for roads, toll-houses, road material. Divisional Council can acquire. Act 9, 1858, sects. 10, 46, 47; Act 10, 1864, sect. 3.

LANDS, Crown. Acts relating to—2, 1860; 19, 1864; 4, 1867; 5, 1870; 8, 1874; 10, 1874; 14, 1878.

LASHES or corporal punishment of any sort, in NO case to be inflicted until proceedings have been returned approved. Act 14, 1874, sect. 6. See also Act 21, 1876, sect. 5.   Vol. 4, p. 406.   p. 291.

LAW. General Amendment Act, 8 of 1879.

———— of Evidence. Ordinances 72, 1830, and 14, 1846. Act 4, 1861.

LAWFUL excuse, proof of, on persons found loitering. Act 23, 1879, sect. 4.

———— Proof of, on person having in possession housebreaking implements. Act 27, 1882, sect. 8.

———— excuse made under Vagrancy Act. Buchanan, part 4, p. 214.

LEASE of land no longer void, or voidable on account of un-
productiveness, tempest, &c., nor rent irrecoverable by such
reason, or because lessor has absolute need of such land,
unless such conditions have been absolutely stipulated.
Act 8, 1879, sect. 4.

———— Landlord's liability for defects. Buchanan, part 4, p. 233.

———— of settled estates. Act 17, 1876.

LEGAL title of Divisional Council to sue and to be sued.
Act 4, 1865, sect. 70.

———— opinion or assistance in management of insolvent estate,
trustees may obtain. Ordinance 6, 1843, sect. 58.

———— adviser or friend of prisoner may have free access after
committal for trial, subject to regulations of R. M., but not
before, except by express authority of magistrate. Ordinance 40, 1828, sect. 38.

———— tender, silver is. Also twelve pence in copper. Ordinance 2, 1825.

LESSEES of crown lands liable for road rates and eligible
as members of Divisional Council if paying £30 and over.
Act 3, 1870, sect. 3.

LETTERS of administration.

———— of credit. Holders of bills who held them over and filled
in dates, how entitled to recover. Buchanan, 1875, part 4, p. 152.

LEVIES. Persons enrolled in, are not entitled to carry arms.
Act 4, 1879.

LIBEL, or defamatory libel (q. v.). Act 46, 1882. Magistrate
has no jurisdiction in (criminal) libel, unless case remitted
by A. G. or S. G. Sect. 9.

———— Evidence as to truth of libel cannot be led at preliminary
examination. See case in E. D. Court. *Shaw and Fennell
v. Bayne, N. O.*, reported Cape Law Journal.

———— Publication of libel. Buchanan, 1875, part 3, p. 93.

———— Damages recovered against newspaper editor, publish-
ing, as advertisement, a letter criticising plaintiff's acts.
Buchanan, 1875, part 4, p. 145.

———— Discovery sought and refused. Defendant wished to justify after plaintiff had joined issue. Buchanan,1876, part 2, p.82.

———— Newspaper comments. Libellous articles put on defendant the onus of proving that the occasion was privileged,
or comments only *bonâ fide* on conduct of a public man.
Buchanan, 1879, part 4, p. 240.

LICENCE, penalty for selling without ; five times the amount
of (does not apply to joint stock companies). Act 3, 1864,
sect. 23. Retail shops. Ordinance 11, 1846.

———— wine and spirits. Act 28, 1883.

LICENCES.

IV. The licences authorized to be granted under this Act shall be
issued by the distributors of stamps, respectively, in Cape Town, and
in the several districts of the colony, and such distributors shall, in
regard to the issue of such licences, and any privileges allowed or granted
to the holders thereof, to be noted or endorsed upon any licence, conform
to the provisions of this Act, and any regulations to be made by the
Governor relating to the performance of their duties under this Act.

Vol. 3, p. 157.

p. 568.

S. Law, p. 362.

ib. pp. 82, 84.

S. Law, p. 267.

V. For or in respect of licences granted or renewed, or transfers or removals of licences or privileges allowed to the holders of licences under and in terms of this Act there shall be payable and paid to the public such sums of money to be collected by means of stamps as are prescribed in the schedule hereto.

VI. Licences under this Act may be granted of the several descriptio̅ following, that is to say :—
(1) Wholesale Licences, (2) Retail Licences, (3) Bottle Licences, (4) Temporary Licences, (5) Club Licences.

VII. In regard to licences granted under this Act the following definitions and provisions shall apply:

DISQUALIFICATIONS.

VIII. No licence shall be granted or transferred to any person or to the wife of any person.
(1) Holding office or appointment under government;
(2) Occupying premises of which any constable or member of a police force is the proprietor or landlord, or in which such constable or member has any interest;
(3) Convicted of selling liquor without a licence until after a period of one year subsequent to the date of such conviction;
(4) Licensed to sell or otherwise deal in diamonds or keeping a native eating house in any district in which the Diamond Trade Act of 1882 is or shall hereafter be in operation.

LICENCE to deal in gunpowder, £3. Ordinance 7, 1834.
LICENCES. Restrictions on the issue of new.

RESTRICTIONS UPON THE ISSUE OF NEW LICENCES.

XXIII. The voters registered for the election of members of Parliament within the limits of any field-cornetcy, municipality divided into wards, within the limits of any ward, may, not less than four days before the annual meeting of the licensing court, lodge with the resident magistrate of that district in which such voters reside, a memorial or memorials objecting to the increase of the number of licenced premises for the sale of liquor under any retail licence or bottle licence or under licences of both descriptions within the limits of such field-cornetcy, municipality, or place, or ward of a municipality as the case may be.

XXIV. With respect to every such memorial the following provisions shall apply:—
(1) It may be in the form marked A in the third Schedule, or to the like effect.
(2) It shall contain the name in full of every voter signing the same, corresponding to the name as registered on the list of registered voters, and his place of residence or business.
(3) Annexed or suspended to such memorial there shall be a declaration signed by the person by whom the signatures were collected in the form as nearly as is material marked B in the said third Schedule.

XXV. Any person who shall
(1) Falsely append the name of any other voter to any such memorial; or
(2) Make any declaration in form or in substance corresponding to the form marked B in the said third Schedule containing any wilfully false statement, shall be liable, upon conviction, to a penalty not exceeding fifty pounds, and in default of payment to imprisonment with or without hard labour for any period not exceeding six months, or to both such penalty and such imprisonment.

XXVI. The resident magistrate receiving any such memorial shall cause the names appearing thereon to be compared with the list of registered voters, and he may strike off therefrom any names which are either illegible, or do not appear in the list of registered voters, or do not correspond with any name in such list, and shall ascertain and certify the number of names of registered voters appearing properly to be appended to such memorial: Provided that any person whose name has been so struck off may appear in person before the resident magistrate, or before the licensing court, and upon satisfying such magistrate or court that he is a registered voter, and signed the said memorial, his name may be restored: and any person may, in like manner, appear and have his name withdrawn, or, if forged or improperly appended, struck off.

XXVII If it shall appear that such a majority (as hereinafter mentioned) of the voters registered within the limits of the field-cornetcy or other locality in question object to the grant of any new licence increasing the number of licensed premises as aforesaid, then it shall not be competent for the licensing court to grant any certificate which shall have the effect of increasing the number of licensed premises of the description referred to in the memorial or memorials.

(1) During one year then ensuing, if such majority shall exceed one-half of the voters then registered within such limits.

LICENSING Courts constituted. Act 28, 1883.

LICENSING COURTS.

XXVIII. A Court for the consideration and determination of applications for or relating to the granting, renewal or transfer of licences for the sale of intoxicating liquors is hereby constituted, and shall be held in and for each district of the colony.

Such Court shall consist of

(1) The resident magistrate, or in the absence of the resident magistrate, the assistant resident magistrate (if any).

(2) The mayor, or chairman of any or each municipality within the district, unless disqualified, under the provisions of this Act, and in case such mayor or chairman shall be disqualified, the council or commissioners of the municipality may elect one of their number instead.

(3) Three members of the divisional council of the division which includes such district, to be chosen in the manner provided by this Act.

(4) Such justices of the peace, not being more than two in number, as the Governor may appoint to be members; Provided that no justice of the peace being in the Civil Service shall be so appointed, or shall continue to be a member if he shall enter the Civil Service after appointment.

XXIX. The following persons shall be disqualified for election or appointment, or if elected or appointed, of continuing, as members of a licensing court, that is to say:

(1) The holder of any licence for the sale of intoxicating liquors.

(2) Any brewer or distiller, other than an agriculturist distilling only from fruit the produce of his own property or purchased by him.

(3) Any person interested or concerned in partnership with any holder of such licence as aforesaid, or with any brewer or distiller.

(4) Any paid officer, or agent of any co-partnership or society interested in the sale or the prevention of the sale of intoxicating liquors.

S. Law, p. 553.

LIEN in insolvency. Creditor holding, to state amount of debt due to him. Ordinance 6, 1843, sect. 30.

LIQUID cases. Jurisdiction of R. M. extended to £100, in action founded on bill of exchange, or promissory note, or other written acknowledgment of debt not a mortgage bond. Act 21, 1876, sect. 2.

R. of C., p. 289.

LIQUOR, definition of. Act 28, 1883.

III. In this Act, if not inconsistent with the context:

"Intoxicating liquor" or "liquor" means any spirits, wine, ale, beer, porter, cider, perry, or other fermented, distilled, spirituous or malt liquor of an intoxicating nature, and every drink with which any such liquor shall have been mixed.

"Licence" means any licence for the sale of liquors granted under this or any other Act now or hereafter to be in force relating to the sale of such liquors.

"Licensing court" or "court" means the licensing court of the district wherein a licence is intended to take effect.

LISTS and qualifications of jurors. Ordinance 84, 1831; Act 2, 1876.

LOANS to public bodies. Act 11, 1882.

LOCATIONS. Native. Act 28, 1883.

NATIVE LOCATIONS AND AREAS.

XX. No licence shall be issued for the sale of liquor within the limits of any native location established or to be established under the provisions of the "Native Locations Act, 1876," or the "Native Locations Amendment Act, 1878," or any Act hereafter to be passed for regulating native locations except with the permission of the Governor.

.XXI. In districts where aboriginal natives of South Africa are located or resident, or are congregated upon public or other works or mines, the Governor may define areas within the limits of which it shall not be competent for any licensing court to authorize the grant of a licence for the sale of liquor except with the permission of the Governor. Any licence issued in contravention of this and the last preceding section shall be void.

XXII. Save and except as to any liquor administered medicinally no person shall sell, supply, or give to any aboriginal native any liquor within the limits of any native location or area proclaimed as aforesaid. Any person who shall sell, supply, or give liquor in contravention of this section shall be liable upon conviction to the same penalties and forfeiture of licence, respectively, as are provided for selling liquor without licence.

—— Native. Acts 6, 1876; 8, 1878.   Vol. 5, pp. 151, 349.

LŒSIO enormis. Contract not voidable on account of. Act 8, 1879, sect. 8.   Vol. 6.

LORD'S day. Observance of. Ordinance 1, 1838.

LOTTERIES prohibited. 1789.   S. Law, p. 17.

LUNATICS. Dangerous, care of. Act 20, 1879.

MAGAZINE for gunpowder. Ordinance 7, 1834.   S. Law, p. 352.

—— for private gunpowder. Keeper to be appointed. To take oath, sect. 8; and keep proper accounts (and render them) sect. 9.   p. 355.

MAGISTRATE'S Court Acts. 20 of 1856; 9 of 1857; 12 of 1860; 12 of 1869; 21 of 1876.

—— assistant. Act 16, 1882.

—— and senior clerk. Power of Circuit Court to cancel stamps extended to Act 16, 1876, sect. 1.   Vol. 5, p. 179.

—— of Circuit Court District may, upon affidavit, &c., issue process of Circuit Court to compel appearance of defendant before; or for attachment of property in any suit or action in Circuit Court. Rules of Sup. Court, 164.   R. of C., p. 101.

—— cannot give costs in proceedings under £1. Ordinance Act 31 of 1875, notwithstanding. Buchanan, 1879, part 1, p. 13.

—— has discretionary power to amend pleadings in civil cases. Buchanan, 1879, part 2. See also sect. 50, Act 20 of 1856.   p. 119.

—— has judicial discretion as to costs. Buchanan, 1879, part 4, p. 232.

—— to aid and assist in insolvent cases. Ordinance 6, 1843, sect. 15.   S. Law, p. 544.

—— to take oaths of office. Tennant's R. of C.   pp. 172, 205. · p. 173.

—— Court to be a Court of Record.

MAIN Roads Act, 9, 1859. Powers of Road Boards transferred to Divisional Councils. Act 10 of 1864.

MAIN through municipality. Council and municipality to repair. *Ibid.* Sect. 12.

Vol. 3, p. 45.

MAJORITY fixed at 21 years of age. Ordinance 62, 1849, sect. 1. By the operation of our law, however, persons come to their majority sooner if "emancipated" from parental control. See "Infant."

S. L., p. 143.

MALICE. Culpable negligence in swearing to facts, without knowing whether they are false or true. Evidence of. 1 Juta 4. 4th ed. 'Addison on Torts.'

pp. 274–268.
p. 625.
p. 273.

—— Definition of. 1 Juta 4. Sup. C. Reports.

MALICIOUS prosecution. Case dropping for want of a prosecutor action was brought for. Magistrate's dismissal of action sustained. 1 Juta 3, p. 178.

—— Arrest, ways of. Reasonable and probable cause is malice. 1 Juta 4, p. 267.

—— prosecution : is where a person acting maliciously and without reasonable or probable cause has preferred against another in a criminal Court or before a judicial officer, a charge which in the event has been declared to be false, but which during its pendency has inflicted some injury to the person, property, or reputation of plaintiff. *Essential conditions.*—1. A criminal charge must have been preferred before a judicial officer. Any act by which the law is set in motion will not amount to malicious prosecution. "There can be no malicious prosecution until the parties come before a Court or a judicial officer" (per Wills J. L. R. 5, C. P. 540). 2. The charge must have been false in fact and so determined by the proper criminal Court before which it came finally; because although the first Court may have decided against plaintiff, it is enough if Court of Appeal decided in his favour. The reversal of conviction is necessary in every case except for malicious exhibition of articles of the peace.

MARITIME and Mercantile Law to be English. Act 8, 1879.

MARKETS. Produce need not necessarily pass through. Ordinance 20, 1847.

—— Master can sell on market articles for which otherwise special licence is required by virtue of Ordinance 9, 1836.

p. 180.

Buchanan, 1879, part 3, p. 180.

S. Law, p. 446.

MARRIAGE. Ordinance 183; Act 16, 1860.

Vol. 6, p. 398.

—— licences. Act 9, 1882.

—— of widow or widower. See "Inheritance of Minors."

—— Sect. 5. Marriage lawfully contracted by the Dutch Roman law, and not preceded by an ante-nuptial contract, creates a partnership between husband and wife, under the sole administration of the husband, in all property, movable or immovable, belonging to either of them before the marriage, or coming to either during the marriage until the date of its dissolution. The idea of separate property is entirely excluded, and a perfect community exists. The wife's position is assimilated to that of a minor, her husband being her guardian, *she cannot sue or be sued.* She cannot contract, except upon the principles on which minors are sometimes permitted to contract. But the husband's power over the property brought by his wife into the community is far greater than that of a guardian over the property of his ward ; as the sole administrator of all, both his and hers, he may, *stante matrimonia*, alienate and encumber at will, without her consent, all property, movable and immovable, vested in her before the marriage, or which she may have acquired during the marriage, in like manner as he may encumber or alienate what had belonged to him before the marriage or had come to him during its subsistence. In effect, the partnership is carried on in the sole name and under the sole control of the husband. (See also Maasdorp's ' Grotius,' Book 1, chap. 5, sect. 23, page 26.) On the other hand a married woman ... may not alienate or encumber her husband's property or her own.

MARRIED Women, suits by. See "Unions"; also "Marriage."

MASTERS and Servants. Objection to jurisdiction. Piece workman. 1 Juta 4, p. 253. Sect. 14, Act 18, 1873.

────── Shepherd failing to preserve part of goat that died not punishable except when he shall have general instructions to this effect. 1 Juta 5, p. 409.

────── Offence under Act must be charged as contravention of special paragraph and section.

────── First conviction does not expose to imprisonment without option of fine. E. D. C. R., 2 Buchanan 4, p. 191.

────── Defendant cannot be sentenced to both fine and imprisonment under Act. E. D. C. R., 2 Buchanan 2, p. 161.

────── Act 7, 1875. Master deposing that to secure attendance Vol. 5, p. 81. of any servant, it is necessary to arrest, R. M. or J. P. may issue warrant. Penalty for malicious deposition not exceeding £5, or one month *without* hard labour. No warning necessary. *Ibid.* Sect. 1.

────── Desertion from service with intent not to return. Warrant may be issued. *Ibid.* Sect. 2.

────── Abusive or insulting language under sect. 8, part 9, Act 18, 1873. *Ibid.* Sect. 3.

────── Evidence of master, servant, &c., and his or their wife, competent witnesses but not compellable. *Ibid.* Sect. 4.

────── Accused not actually in custody not to be placed in the dock except at discretion of magistrate. *Ibid.* Sect. 5.

────── Persons employed on public works may be prosecuted by officer in charge. *Ibid.* Sect. 6.

────── Act 15, 1856, vol. 1, page 106. Definition of servant. Any person employed for hire, wages or other remuneration to perform any handicraft, or other bodily labour in agriculture or manufactories, or in domestic service, or as a boatman, porter, or the like. *Ibid.* Sect. 2.

────── Act, 15, 1856, vol. 1, page 106 ; sects. 3, 4, 5, 6, 7, 8, 9, 16, 17, 18, 19, 20, 21, 22, 23, 25, 26 of 5th chap. repealed by, and anything repugnant to Act 18, 1873, Act 18, 1873. Vol 4, p. 293. ────── No contract of service valid for more than one year, nor any contract valid unless service to commence within one month from date of contract, unless made before R. M. or other proper officer. R. M. to satisfy himself that that servant enters into contract voluntary and with clear understanding of effect, and shall then attest it. *Ibid.*

MASTERS and Servants. Offences by agricultural servants. Sects. 2, 3, 4 and 5. *Ibid.*

———— No fine paid or imprisonment undergone to cancel contract. *Ibid.* Sect. 6.

———— Sects. 2, 3, 4, 5, 6, 9, only to apply to agricultural servants, and not then to servants under 16 years of age. *Ibid.* Sect. 7.

———— Offences by domestic servants; fine £2, or one month. Hard labour cannot be given. R. M. may assess damage done by servant. Sect. 15, chap. 5. Act 15, 1856. *Ibid.* Sect. 7.

———— Complaints must be lodged within one month. *Ibid.* Sect. 8.

———— Agricultural servants may be warned to attend before R. M. at any reasonable time, and not obeying, may, on affidavit that he received warning, and has no lawful cause for not appearing, be arrested on warrant. If convicted may be ordered to pay costs of master, if warned also by summons that costs will be asked for against him. *Ibid.* Sect. 9.

———— Complainant failing to appear, defendant may get an order for costs of self and material witnesses. Complainant in default failing to pay, may be fined £5, or one month's hard labour. *Ibid.* Sect. 10.

———— Servant complaining against master, and failing to appear, same procedure and penalty as above. *Ibid.* Sect. 11.

———— Servant may leave service to lodge complaints, even after leave refused, and shall not be treated as deserting or contravening Act. *Ibid.* Sect. 12.

———— Servant accused under 2nd or 4th section may be convicted under 4th or 2nd, as the proof may go, penalty to be according to 2nd section only. Servant to have notice of nature of charge. *Ibid.* Sect. 13.

———— Withholding wages without cause, fine £5, and in default imprisonment without hard labour for one month, and be condemned to pay wages due and costs of proceedings as costs in civil cases, and such wages and costs may be levied on property of master. Judgment may be given for wages only, and costs as R. M. may direct. *Ibid.* Sect. 14.

———— Detaining unlawfully any animals of servant, fine £1 for each animal, but no more than £5 in all, or one month without hard labor, and R. M. shall order delivery of animals with costs, as in civil cases. Costs leviable. Nothing herein to impair lawful contract giving a right to detain animals. *Ibid.* Sect. 15.

———— Failure to find food, bedding, or articles stipulated for, or such food, &c., not conformable to contract, fine £5 or one month without hard labour. *Ibid.* Sect. 16.

———— Contract may be cancelled by R. M. in any suit by servant against master, if servant shall desire, on proof that master has not fairly performed his part. *Ibid.* Sect. 17.

MASTERS and Servants. Costs of actions to be at public expense except when brought without reasonable or probable cause, when party complaining liable to fine of £5 and costs of suit or one month (no H. L.). *Ibid.* Sect. 18.

———— Fines paid to Treasury. *Ibid.* Sect. 19.

———— Contract of service may be set aside by R. M. if fraud or misrepresentation induced either party to enter into. Act 15, 1856, sect. 3.   Vol. 1, p. 108.

———— Acts 15, 1856; 18, 1873; 7, 1875.

———— See Wrongful dismissal. Buchanan, 1879, part 1, p. 22.

———— A stationer's assistant is not a servant under these acts.

MEASURES and Weights. Acts 11, 1858 and 15, 1876.

———— Unit of land measure. Act 9, 1859.

MEDDLING with property of insolvent when attached.   S. Law, p. 544.

MEDICAL. Ordinance 82, 1830. No person to practice without licence. To submit diploma to Government. Sect. 3. Penalty. Sect. 5.

———— man dispensing his own drugs to take out licence as apothecary.

MEDICINES. Every wholesale and retail licence authorizes sale of patent, homœopathic and "Dutch" medicines. Act 15, 1877.   Vol. 5, p. 244.

MEETING of creditors. How called (1st and 2nd).   S. L., p. 549.

———— Election of trustee at 2nd.

———— Before whom held.   p. 551.

———— General. Trustee can call at any time.   p. 568.

———— in Cape Town before Master; in country before Magistrate. Sect. 57.

———— Insolvent to attend, unless leave given by Master or R. M., and also whenever notice given, to answer questions and give account of estate, deliver up papers, &c. *Ibid.*

———— of Divisional Council. Quorum to be five (without C. C.). Act 25, 1869, sect. 2.   Acts, vol. 4, p. 24.

———— Public, when legal. Ordinance 15, 1848.

MEMBER of Divisional Council vacates seat by resignation, insolvency, assigning estate, entering civil or military service, absenting himself from three regular monthly meetings. Acts 4, 1865.   Vol. 3, p. 155.

MERCHANDIZE, Fraudulent marking of. Act 12, 1864.

MERCHANT Seaman's Acts 13, 1855; 3, 1863; 13, 1874.

MESSENGER, Court of R. M. To take oath of office, to give security to satisfaction of R. M. Act 20, 1856, rules 4 and 5.   R. of C., p. 206.

MILEAGE under Pound Ordinance. 4d. per mile not exceeding 10 miles, going, and same returning. Sect. 5. Above 10 miles 3d. per mile. If necessary for proper care of animals, more persons than one may be employed. *Ibid.* Ordinance 16, 1847.   S. Law, p. 828.

MINING Leases Act 9, 1877.   Vol. 5, p. 233.

MINORS or Married Women, suits by. Act 20, 1856, sect. 51. See also "Marriage."

MINORS carrying on trade, and living apart from parents, acquire persona standi in judicio, in action for money lent. Buchanan, 1876, part 1, p. 5.

—— minority is not a defence to promissory note, when minor traded with consent of Tutor Dative. Buchanan, 1879, part 3, p. 147.

—— cannot be punished for neglect of duty under contract to which father (or natural guardian) was not a party. Buchanan, 1879, part 4, p. 288.

—— parent is not answerable for tort committed by. Grotius 3. 1. 34. Voet. 15. 1. 11. Buchanan, E. D. C. R.

MISCONDUCT of Servant. Defence in action for wrongful dismissal. Buchanan, 1879, part 4.

p. 217.

MISJOINDER of defendant (plea in abatement) over-ruled. Buchanan, 1876, part 2, p. 62.

MONEY lent or paid. Plea of general issue. Defendant may prove under this plea that loan or payment was made without any implied promise to repay, or that a contract was made inconsistent with the indebitatus contract—viz., that he received money for lending his name to plaintiff as endorser of promissory note, &c.

MORTGAGE Bond.   Provisional sentence on refused. Buchanan, 1879, part 4, p. 206.

MUNICIPAL Irrigation. Act 28, 1879.

—— Meeting. Magistrate, may call, on receiving requisition from 25 resident householders on three weeks' notice.

S. Law, p. 389.

—— limits. Land within, not to be treated as waste crown land. Act 14, 1878.

Vol. 5, p. 384.

—— Regulations. Contraventions of. See Act 12, 1878, sects. 16 or 18 (Grahamstown only).

—— Regulations do not oust common law rights, i.e. plaintiff has a right to sue for trespass under common law, although there be a municipal regulation. 1 Juta 4, p. 288.

MUNICIPALITY can impose dog tax.   1875, part 3, page 101.

—— cannot tax crown property. 1879, part 3, page 169.

—— Laws of, consolidated. Act 45, 1882.

May have additional police appointed on paying one half expense. Act 15, 1857.

Acts, vol. 1, p. 235.

Meeting of householders must decide, and municipality intimate to R. M. the desire. *Ibid.* Sect. 1.

Magistrate to ascertain number of force and frame detailed estimate. *Ibid.* Sect. 2.

Report particulars to Government. *Ibid.* Sect. 3.

Government may reduce number or cost. Governor shall signify approval in writing to R. M. *Ibid.* Sect. 4.

To call meeting of householders to procure funds for police rate. *Ibid.* Sect. 5.

When half cost paid to R. M. he shall nominate policemen for approval of Governor. *Ibid.* Sect. 6.

Police to come under police ordinance. *Ibid.* Sect. 7.

Annual account of expenditure shall be furnished to

municipality by R. M., *Ibid.*, Sect. 8, and municipality shall pay one half of cost in advance.

Should expenditure be less then estimate, government will refund and vice versa. *Ibid.* Sect. 9.

To give three months' notice of cessation. *Ibid.* Sect. 10.

Neglect to do so, lawful to employ policemen for three months. *Ibid.* Sect. 11.

Number of policemen may be reduced or added to. Provisions of sect. 9 and 10 to apply to sect. 12.

Ordinance 9 of 1836 amended by Act 13, 1864. Vol. 3, p. 65.

Election of Commissioners to be triennial, from 1st March, 1865, viz.: 1868, 1871, 1874, 1877, 1880, 1883, 1886, 1889, 1892, 1895, 1898, 1901, 1904, &c. *Ibid.* Sect. 3.

Casual vacancy. Commissioner to go out of office on next triennial election. *Ibid.* Sect. 4.

If from failure or neglect, meeting to elect shall not be duly or regularly holden, three or more resident householders to notify R. M. or J. P., who shall call a meeting by notice of not less than 7 or more than 14 days in the manner prescribed by Order 9, 1836. Commissioners in office to remain until their successors have been elected. *Ibid.* Sect. 5.

Qualification of voters : Occupier of house, warehouse, counting house, shop or office at rent not less than £10. Voter to have only one vote. *Ibid.* Sect. 7.

Joint occupiers of tenements, value of each not less than £10, regarded as separate householders. *Ibid.* Sect. 8.

Contracts with municipality, no Commissioner may have. Shareholders in joint stock companies may hold office, although company are contractors. *Ibid.* Sect. 9.

Rate not to exceed one penny in the pound. Commissioners may assess once a year, four-fifths of Commissioners to be present and to consent to rate. *Ibid.* Sect. 10. Acts, vol. 3. p. 68.

Rate, whether payable by occupier or by proprietor, commissioners may fix. *Ibid.* Sect. 11.

Appeal against valuation for rate to Court of R. M. Decision final. *Ibid.* Sect. 13.

Fines imposed for breach of regulations payable to municipality. *Ibid.* Sect. 15. Ordinances 9, 1836 ; 2, 1844 ; 8, 1848 ; and Act 15, 1860.

MURDER. Private persons may apprehend for. Ordinance 73, 1830, sects. 14 and 15. R. of C., page 376.

—— indictment for. See "Indictment."

MUTUAL credits allowed to set off by Master or R. M. at meeting of creditors. Ordinance 6, 1843, sect. 28. S. L., p. 552.

—— appeal against, allowed. *Ibid.* p. 553.

NAME idem sonaus. Buchanan, 1879, part 2, page 43.

NATIVE children. Importation of, prevented.

—— Sanction of Governor to be obtained for the introduction of child under 16 years of age. Fine £20 and 1s. 6d. per diem for every day in which child kept.

Acts, vol. 1, pp. 264–5. **NATIVE** governor to be guardian. Except persons on journey, certificate to be given by R. M. Act 22, 1857.

Vol. 5, p. 151. —— location, supervision of. Act 6 of 1876.

—— governor may appoint inspector. Location to consist of not less than 100 houses, unless on private persons' ground. Inspector may have charge of more locations than one. *Ibid.* Sect. 1.

—— inspector's salary to be paid out of revenue, but natives on locations to pay one-half. *Ibid.* Sect. 2.

—— or natives one-quarter, and private persons on whose land, the remaining one-quarter.

—— R. M. may summon persons having no right on location and order him to remove ; if disobedient, may be summarily removed by inspector or constable. *Ibid.* Sect. 12.

—— Court of R. M. to have jurisdiction over all offenders on. *Ibid.* Sect. 16. Act 8, 1878, vol. 5, p. 349 ; Act 40, 1879. Governor may divide location into lots and let on quit-rent.

—— Succession Act, 18, 1864, vol. 3. Buchanan, E. D. Court, vol. 1, part 2, p. 195. Passes Law Act 22, 1867 (11th sect. repealed).

NEGATIVE servitude. Cannot be acquired by prescription unless there has intervened some act of assertion by person claiming it and the party opposed has yielded. Buchanan, 1879, part 2, page 79.

NEGLIGENCE as attorney, renders himself liable in damages. Buchanan, 1875, part 4, page 133.

—— of plaintiff or defendant, when injury done, a considerable factor. Buchanan, 1879, part 1, page 8.

NIGHT. Persons found with face blacked or wearing felt or other slippers, or being disguised with criminal intent. Act 27 of 1882. Sect. 8, part 2.

—— Persons found at—without lawful excuse (proof on such persons) in or upon any dwelling house, warehouse, coachhouse, stable, cellar, or outhouse, enclosed yard, garden or area, or on board any ship or vessel lying in port or harbour. *Ibid.* Sect. 8, part 3.

NOMINATION of candidate for Divisional Council. Act 4,

Vol. 3, p. 141. 1865, sect. 19.

NON-APPEARANCE or non-attendance of witnesses. In *Civil* cases, Rule 18, page 212. Fine £5 or 14 days ; if duly summoned and expenses paid. Warrant may be issued. In *Criminal* cases. Rule 75, page 241. Same fine. Absence of material witness in civil cases, R. M. may hear evidence and postpone, or postpone without taking any evidence. Act 20, 1856, Rule 19, page 212.

NON-JOINDER. In trespass — of owner—exception disallowed. Buchanan, 1875, part 4, page 136.

—— plea of—and leave to amend declaration with costs. Buchanan, 1879, part 2, page 117.

NOTARIAL presentation. Not necessary when note made

' payable at place of business of plaintiff—in action against maker.

NOTARIAL protest. Not necessary against maker, where note made payable at a particular place.

—— protest not necessary on note under £20 in R. M. Court. Act 20, 1856. Sect. 9.   S. L., p. 174.

NOT GUILTY. Objections under plea of — 1st. That crime is not one punishable by law ; 2nd. That facts charged in indictment do not amount, in law, to offence charged ; 3rd. Exception to relevancy of indictment in any material point. 4th. That it appears by indictment, that offence is barred by prescription. R. of C., page 82, Rule 92.

NOTICE of trial. Trial by jury. Buchanan, 1876, part 2, page 63.   S. L., p. 568.

—— of meetings in insolvent estates in Gazette. Insolvent Ordinance, 1843, sect. 56.

NOTICES of Divisional Council published in Gazette. Act 4, 1865.   Vol. 3, p. 161.

—— without charge to council, see " Government Gazette."

NUISANCE in thoroughfares, roads, &c. Act 27, 1882, sect. 7.

—— in shambles, outhouse, yard, lane, alley, &c. Inspecting constable by order of R. M. may order abatement · of nuisance—if not done after four days, penalties imposed. *Ibid.* Sect. 13.

—— Act 2, 1855. Discharge of firearms not punishable if for lawful purposes. Buchanan, 1879, part 3, page 131.

—— Any one of the public can proceed to obtain interdict to abate public, 1879, part 1, page 2.

OATH by valuators of Divisional Council. Act 10, 1864, sect. 36.   Vol. 3, p. 51

—— by members of Court for valuation. *Ibid.*

—— substituting declarations for. Ordinance 6, 1846.

—— as Res. Mag. R. of C., pp. 172 & 205. Act. 20, 1856. Schedule A, sect. 6.

—— of messenger of the Court of Res. Mag. Act 20, 1856, Rule 4. R. of C., page 206.

—— of witnesses in R. M. Court. *Ibid.* Rule 20, page 213.

OFFENCES, prosecution of all, except murder, barred by prescription after expiration of 20 years. Libel after six months from date of publication. Act 46, 1882, sect. 10.

—— under Act 27 of 1882. Persons committing, may be summarily arrested without warrant by constable, or by owner of the property or his servant. Act 27, 1882, sect. 18.

—— on or near boundaries. Ordinance 73, 1830, and Act 7, 1873.

—— committed on boundary of division triable by either R. M. Sect. 44, page 192.

OFFENDERS, Juvenile. Act 21, 1869.

OLD council to remain until new one properly elected and published. Act 4, 1864, sect. 50.

ONE witness—sufficient in *Civil* cases. Ordinance 72, 1830, · sect. 32.   S. L., p. 419.

ONE witness sufficient in *Criminal* cases except for perjury, when other evidence of "guilty" must be adduced. *Ibid.* Sect. 33.

OPINION, legal. Trustee may take—and charge fee to estate, or employ an attorney. Statute Law, page 568, sect. 58.

ORAL contract of service not binding for more than one year, and not then unless stipulated that service shall commence within one month from date of contract. Act 15, 1856, chapter 2, sect. 3.

Vol. 1, p..109.

ORDINANCE relating to Divisional Council, pound and trespass ordinance. Ordinance 16, 1847. See " P."

Vol. 4, p. 86.

OSTRICHES, wild, preservation of. Act 12, 1870.

Proclamation 21 March 1822 as far as relating to ostrich eggs repealed. Sect. 1.

Vol. 4, p. 86.

———— License to kill wild ostriches. Penalty for killing without, first offence, £30 to £40 ; every subsequent offence £40 to £100 ; any person convicted within six months from date of offence may be imprisoned with or without hard labour for six months in default of payment. Sect. 2.

Vol. 4, p. 86.

License to kill or catch, £20. No person, licensed or not, to kill ostrich in breeding season. Sect. 4.

Vol. 4, p. 87.

Governor may fix fence or breeding season (close season). Sect. 3.

Vol. 4, p. 86.

Fines not exceeding £50 may be recovered in R. M. Court, subject to review by Superior Courts. Sect. 5.

Vol. 4, p. 87.

Informer at discretion of Court to receive not less than £1 or more than £5. Sect. 8.

Vol. 4, p. 87.

Governor may proclaim certain districts as protected for a term of years. Penalty for contravening proclamation to be as in II. section. Sect. 9.

Vol. 4, p. 88.

Absence of name from list of licences *primâ facie* evidence of accused not being licensed to kill. Sect. 10.

Vol. 4, p. 88.

Vol. 5, p 101.

———— preservation of, Act 15, 1875. Owner or occupier of land may catch and keep young ostriches (not two months old) or the eggs of ostriches found on his land, without a licence. Sect. 2. Any other person so offending, i.e. without a licence, taking or having in his possession, destroying or disturbing any wild ostrich eggs. Penalty not exceeding £10 for each egg, if information laid within six months. On conviction and being in default of payment, *imprisonment* with or without hard labour for not exceeding 12 months. Sect. 1, p. 101, vol. 5.

———— Wild, protection of. Act 12, 1870 and 15, 1875. *Tame* and *domesticated.* Act 10, 1871, *repealed.*

If tame and kept within enclosure and escaping, same property in owner as in an ox or any other domesticated animal. Any criminal offence for killing, injuring, or " converting " may be tried as usual. Act 24, 1875, sect. 1.

Vol. 5, p. 126.

Dogs found in enclosures may be destroyed by owner or occupier. Malicious destruction of dog exposes to action for damages. (R. M. Court may try.) *Ibid.* Sect. 2.

Act does not take away any ordinary right of action for trespass, injury or prevent prosecution of any offence. *Ibid.* Sect. 4.

OSTRICHES. Brought under pounds and trespass laws. Act 31, 1875, sect. 1. Vol. 5, p. 144.
—— Pound fees for ostriches, see schedule to Act as above.
Wild. Protection Act 15, 1875. Removal of eggs by servant of co-proprietor not punishable. Buchanan, 1875, part 4, page 137.
Damages to, by dogs. Owner liable on account of his wrongful act. 1876, part 2, page 161.
Damages to. Owner of dog held liable. Scienter not necessary to be proved. Buchanan, 1876, part 2, page 103. Voet. 9. 1. 6. Grot. 3. 83. 13.
—— pound fees on. Act 31, 1875.
PARTNER, service on one, of firm good. Act 20, 1856. Rule 11.
PARTNERSHIP or joint stock company may in indictment be described by name, style, or firm. Individuals need not be specially named. Act 15, 1864, sect. 2. R. of C., page 401; Limited Liability Act, 24, 1861.
—— not dissolved by death, where deed of partnership provides for continuation of—for the estate of deceased partner. Buchanan, 1879, part 4, page 195. Vol. 3, p. 324.
PASSES. Pass Act, 22 of 1867.
Native foreigner to mean native of any tribe (other than Fingoe) of which principal chief shall live beyond Colony. *Ibid.* Sect. 6.
All Kafirs and Tambookies to have passes, unless possessing certificate of citizenship. Kafirs, &c., residing in the colony (proprietor of land, &c.) not less than 7 years consecutive, Governor may direct certificate may be issued. 27th section of Act 17 of 1864 to apply. *Ibid.* Sect. 7.
J. P., police constable, field cornet, owner or occupier of land, may demand production of pass—and apprehend on failure to produce, or breach of conditions of pass, and bring before R. M. *Ibid.* Page 325.
Fingoe or Kaffir producing certificate shall not be apprehended. *Ibid.* Page 325.
Act 17, 1864, repealed as far as annual revision and renewal of certificate concerned. Wrongful or malicious arrest, without probable cause, punishable by fine of £1 and damages, to be assessed by R. M. before whom case comes on for trial. *Ibid.* Page 326.
To and contracts with natives.
Contracts can be made under master and servants law. *Ibid.* Sect. 2, page 323.
Native foreigner may not enter Colony without a pass signed by officer appointed.
Pass as in schedule A. *Ibid.* Page 326. Penalty. — One month's imprisonment with or without hard labour, or spare diet, or fine of £1 and in default to such imprisonment. *Ibid.* Sect. 3, page 623.
R. M. or pass officer may issue pass or extend period of pass, endorsing permission thereon.
Native violating condition, same penalty as Sect. 3. *Ibid.* Sect. 4, page 323.

PASSES. For contract of service, see " Contract." *Ibid.* Sect. 5, page 324.

PAUPER, action by—in *formâ pauperis*—In Supreme Court, &c. Rules 123 to 130 in R. M. Court.—R. M. may order process to issue without fee or charge. If successful, liable to make them good. Act 20, 1856, Rule 13. R. of C., page 209.

    In case.   Court may order costs to be paid out of money recovered. Buchanan, 1876, part 1, page 39.

PAYMENT to Agent. Power to sell does not, as a general principle, confer right to receive price, but may not be inferred from certain circumstances. 1 Juta 4, page 290.

PEACE Preservation Act 13, 1878, vol. 5, page 374. Governor may proclaim district—no arms, ammunition, &c., to be carried by unlicensed persons. *Ibid.* Sect. 1.

    Proclamation to be gazetted, &c. *Ibid.* Sect. 2.

    Government Gazette to be proof in Court of Law of proclamation. *Ibid.* Sect. 3.

    Persons allowed to carry arms without licence, R. M., J. P., Field Cornet, Naval, Military, Burgher or Volunteer, F. Police or other armed police.

    All persons, including levies, Act. 4, 1879, to give arms up to R. M. *Ibid.* Sect. 4.

    Governor may authorize persons to grant licences. *Ibid.* Sect. 5.

    Dealer in firearms to obtain licence. *Ibid.* Sect. 6.

    On issue of licence owner may receive arms, &c., back again. *Ibid.* Sect. 7.

    On conviction of carrying arms, &c., without a licence, penalty not exceeding £500, or seven years' imprisonment with hard labour. *Ibid.* Sect. 8.

    R. M.,' J. P., constable, or person licensed, may demand (burgher, yeoman, or volunteer) of person carrying arms, his licence, and may arrest without warrant and take to R. M. or nearest J. P. *Ibid.* Sect. 9 and 17.

    R. M., J. P., Field Cornet, Constable, may search suspected persons for arms, without warrant, and seize. *Ibid.* Sect. 10.

    Governor may revoke licence issued, and person must deposit arms, &c. *Ibid.* Sect. 11.

    Making or mending for unlicensed persons prohibited. *Ibid.* Sect. 12.

    Attorney-General or Solicitor-General may remit the case back to R. M. *Ibid.* Sect. 13.

    Register of licences issued to be kept. *Ibid.* Sect. 14.

    Copy of the same to be sent to Colonial Secretary in month of January every year. Definition of Arms. *Assegay included. Ibid.* Sect. 18.

PENALTY on unstamped documents. Stamps may be affixed within 21 days without any penalty. Afterwards 21 to 42 days double duty; 42 days to 62 threefold duty. After 62 days, Governor's consent must be obtained. Act 3, 1864, sect. 14. R. of C., page 297.

Stat. Law, 574, s. 67. ——— for false answers (Insolvent) Perjury.

PENSION. Any public officer, other than a judge, may be pensioned, or required to retire on pension at sixty years of age. Act 4, 1878. Vol. 5, p. 330.

PERENNIAL Streams. Definition of. 1876, part 1, page 25.

PERICULUM rei venditae. 1879, part 2, page 91.

—— Excise duty to be held risk of buyer, constructive delivery of brandy having been made. Buchanan, 1879, pt. 3, p. 167.

PERIODICAL Court. Defendant residing nearer seat of magistracy than Periodical Court not to be summoned before, except by consent. Act 9, 1857, sect. 3. R. of C., page 273.

Appeal within ten days after judgment or sentence. *Ibid.* Sect. 7, page 275.

Process issued by person appointed—by Government Gazette. Shall conform or correspond with Rules of Court of R. M. To be executed by messenger to be appointed by R. M. *Ibid.* Sect. 1, sched. B, page 272.

Clerk and R. M. may issue process and deliver to such messenger. *Ibid.* Sect. 2, page 273.

Criminal Cases. Process under 70th Rule of Court of R. M. may be issued by persons appointed. *Ibid.* Sect. 11, page 276.

Person so appointed may assist in prosecuting, subject to the discretion of R. M. *Ibid.* Sect. 12, page 276.

—— may be held by Assistant Magistrate. Act 11 of 1882, sect. 4.

PERJURY. Two witnesses required to prove—or one credible witness and corroborative evidence of another kind. Ordi- S. Law, p. 419. nance 72, 1830, sect. 32 & 33.

—— Conviction for—sustained, when witness not compellable to answer, but having answered falsely. 1875, part 1, page 6.

—— What is material to charge of—The words alleged to be false should be set forth, and relevancy to some judicial proceeding then pending proved. E. D. C. R., 2 Buchanan, pt. 4, p. 392.

PERPETUAL. Act 10, 1864, made. Act 22, 1873, sect. 7. Vol. 4, p. 303.

PERSONS going around at night. Act 27, 1882, sect. 8, part 4.

—— disqualified as member of Divisional Council. Act 4, 1865, sect. 14.

—— disqualified to hold wine and spirit licence. See Vol. 3, p. 141. " Licence."

PETITION, if adjudged malicious or vexatious. Statute Law, page 546, sect. 19.

PETITIONING Creditor to prosecute sequestration until appointment of trustee. S. Law, p. 539.

—— Costs of—to be first reimbursed out of proceeds.

PHYLLOXERA verstatrix. Act 27, 1880.

PIECE-WORK. Contract may be terminated by master after reasonable time allowed. Act 15, 1856, sect. 2, page 109 ; 1846, sect. 50.

PIGS, poultry, pigeons, trespassing in garden, &c. (see sect.

E 2

32, Ordinance 16, 1847, page 838, S. L., for description of

S. Law, p. 846. place), may be destroyed. Ordinance 16, 1847, sect. 50.

PLAINT. Clerk to R. M. shall enter in record book and shall be taken as plaintiff's declaration. *Ibid.* Page 207.

———— or summons may be amended by R. M. on payment of such costs as Court may deem reasonable. *Ibid.* Page 197, sect. 50.

———— in civil cases in Resident Magistrate's Court. *Ibid.* Pages 244 to 250.

PLAINTIFF has right of reply, Rule 131, page 90, R. of C., except when issue of fact lies with defendant, page 91 R. of Court.

———— or Defendant may appear in civil cases by any person to whom plaintiff or defendant choose to give written power. Such person can make no charge for service on bill of costs unless an advocate, an attorney, or enrolled agent. Act 20, 1856, rule 13, page 209, and 10 R. of C,

PLEA *in abatement.* Leave to amend—48 hours' notice must be given.

———— do. Registered owners of land sufficient in action relating to servitude. 1879, part 2, page 122.

———— of *guilty.* Case remitted under, by Attorney-General. Act 12, 1860, R. of C., page 278.

———— of *not guilty.* Objections to jurisdiction under. See " Not guilty," and Rule of Sup. Court, No. 92. R. of C., p. 82.

PLEAD. If prisoner refuses to plead, Court may enter plea of not guilty. R. of C., pages 81–2, rule 95.

PLEADING. Written notice to plead must be given. 1875, part 1, page 1.

———— Amendment of, at Resident Magistrate's discretion. 1879, part 2, page 119.

PLEADINGS in R. M. Court. Plaintiff need only follow " Forms of Plaint." 1 Juta 3, page 177.

PLEDGED or hypothecated goods. Purchaser of, with know-ledge of pledging. 1879, part 1, page 17.

POISON. Sale of, without written permission from R. M. or prescription by doctor. Penalty not less than £5 and not

S. Law, p. 182. more than £50. Half to informer. Ordinance 82, 1830, sect. 7.

POLICE Force, New. Act 12, 1882. Offences created by, and fines imposed by, may be tried and levied by R. M. *Ibid.* Sect. 43.

———— Refusal to assist. Sect. 13, Ordinance 73–183, page 169; and for penalty, sect. 7, Ordinance 2, 1837.

———— offences. Act 27, 1882.

———— Resistance to, or inciting any person to resist. Hinder-ing or disturbing any constable or officer of local authority in execution of duty. Act 27, 1882, sect. 8, part 5.

———— Divisional, can obtain, by contribution of one-third of

Vol. 4, p. 258. cost. Act 8, 1873, sect. 2.

———— Account of expenditure to be kept. *Ibid.* Sect. 3.

POLICE Acts, 15, 1857 ; 8, 1867 ; 12, 1874.

POSTAGE stamps to be used only for postage. Act 1, Vol. 3, p. 327.
1868.

POSTAGE STAMPS to be used only for Postage. Act 1, Vol. 3, p. 327.
1868.

POSTPONEMENT of trial on affidavit. Act 17, 1874, sect.
3 ; Ordinance 40, 1828, sect. 59.

POUND Ordinance. Prosecution under, does not bar civil
action for damages. Buchanan, 1875, part 2, page 37.

Magistrate cannot give costs in criminal cases under
Ordinance. Act 31, 1875, refers to damages caused by trespass, not to action for rescue or other contravention of
Ordinance. See Act 31, 1875 ; Buchanan, 1879, part 1,
page 13.

———— for pound principle. Act 22, 1873, sect. 3. Vol. 4, p. 301.

POUNDMASTER. To be appointed by C. C. and Divisional
Council. Act 1, 1857, sect. 2.

POUNDS. Acts relating to. Ordinance 16, 1847 ; 1, 1857 ;
21, 1867 ; 1, 1869 ; 31, 1875.

———— and Trespasses Act, 1, 1869. Ordinance 16, 1847, p. 1, vol. 4.
amended. p. 1, sect. I.,
vol. 4.

Stallion over two years old to be castrated unless released p. 1, vol. 4,
under sect. 5. sect. II.

Castration fee 10s., no fee payable if animal die. p. 1, vol. 4,
sect. III.

Stallion must be impounded 5 weeks before castration. p. 1, vol. 4,
Shall be sold after 45 days. If owner consent or decline to sect. IV.
release, the stallion may be castrated at once.

Stallion may be released without castration on owner
paying pound fees and other charges, and giving security
for damages done, under 51st and 55th sections of Ordinance p. 2, vol. 4,
16, 1847. sect. V.
p. 2, vol. 4,
Provisions extended to all municipal pounds. sect. VI.

Act not to be in force until proclaimed by Governer at p. 2, vol. 4,
request of Divisional Council. sect. VII.

Stallion includes mule ass not castrated. p. 2, vol. 4,
sect. VIII.
———— Ostriches brought under provisions of Pounds and
Trespass Law.

Mileage not more than 1s. or less than 4d. per mile.
Pound fees not more than 2s. or less than 1s. for each.
Grazing or herding not more than 2s. or less than 1s. for each.
Trespass money under 32nd sect. of Ordinance 16, 1847, not
more than 3s. for each ; under 33rd sect. not more than one- Vol. 5, p. 144.
third of ordinary rate payable. Act 31, 1875.

Animal trespassing cannot be sold by the owner of the
land. Penalty £20. Owner of animal may also have action Vol. 5, p. 145.
for damages. Sect. 2.

Owner of animal trespassing may tender amount for
damage done before conveyance to pound. Refusal to accept Vol. 5, p. 145.
may expose to loss of costs in action. Sect. 3.

Poundmaster, under penalty of £5 and damages, to
receive all cattle sent by owner or occupier of land, or S. L., p. 828.
under written authority between sunrise and sunset. Sect. 4.

S. L., p. 828, sect. V.
Person bringing to receive mileage 4d. per mile not exceeding 10, coming and same returning. Above 10 miles 3d. More persons than one may be paid if required for safety. See " Civil Commissioner," " Field Cornet," " Divisional Council."

Poundmaster to receive cattle tendered (Statute Law, page 827, sect. 3) by owner or occupier of land or person authorized in writing between sunrise and sunset under penalty of £5 and damages. Poundmaster to give receipt.

Powers vested in Divisional Councils. Act 21, 1867.

May be abolished by C. C. and Divisional Council. Act 1, 1857, sect. 4.

POWERS of Attorney. Execution and attestation of. Act 10, 1879.

Persons granting to sign at foot. Power to be attested by two competent witnesses over 14 years, or by one declaring he was present and saw person sign and acknowledge, or certificate of J. P. and notary.

Declaration as prescribed by Ordinance 6, 1845.

Stamp duties not altered. Act 10, 1879 ; Ordinance 15, 1845; Statute Law, page 745.

PREFERENCE on claim extends to interest. Statute Law, page 559, sect. 33.

PREFERENT and concurrent claims unsatisfied may be brought against fresh sequestration of undischarged insolvent.
S. L., p. 605.
Ordinance 6, 1843, sect. 130.

—— creditor. Right of, not to be interfered with. *Ibid.*
p. 568.
Sect. 56.

PRELIMINARY examination. Magistrate cannot convert proceedings into summary trial. E. D. C. R., 2 Buchanan 4, page 387.

—— Charge of murder remittted to R. M. as case of *Theft.* (Case of Bamberger.) 1 Juta 2, p. 145.

—— examinations. Ordinance 40, 1828, Statute Law, p. 359. To be taken, when R. M. shall consider crime or offence proper for the jurisdiction of a Superior Court. *Ibid.* Sect. 28.

—— All depositions to be taken on oath and in presence of accused in writing, or read over to him and opportunity given by him to cross-examine. *Ibid.* Sect. 31.

—— Magistrate and witnesses to sign. In case of incapacity or refusal, to be signed by two persons in whose presence evidence was given. *Ibid.*

—— for libel. Truth inadmissible as defence at. Witnesses cannot be cross-examined as to the truth of libels.

PREMIUM of Insurance in ante-nuptial contracts. See *ante.*

PRESCRIPTION as regards transfer deed and error found will run from time of discovery of error. 1879, part 1, page 10.

—— Adverse possession to found, must not be " Vi " (by force) " clam " (secret), nor " precario " (at the will and pleasure of another). Juta 1881, vol. 1, part 2, page 124.

PRESCRIPTION. Period of, in criminal cases, R. of C. 357. All crimes except murder must be prosecuted for within 20 years. Ordinance 40, 1828, sect. 21 ; or limitation of time within which action may be brought.   Act 6, 1861.   Vol. 2, p. 233.

———— of promissory notes.   Act 3, 1856.

———— All debts due by child to parent and surety paid by parent for child can be brought into collection although incurred and paid beyond period of prescription.   Buchanan, 1876, part 2, page 92.

———— Longissimmi temporis fixed at 30 years.   Sect. 10, Act 7, 1865.   See 1 Buchanan 2, E. D. C., page 254.

PRESCRIPTIVE right.   30 years' adverse user necessary to prove.   1876, part 3, page 168, Buchanan.

PRESENCE of any person on private premises by night without lawful excuse or on board of ship or vessel.   Act 27, 1882, sect. 8, part 3.

PREVIOUS conviction.   Not competent to sentence to lashes, where previous conviction only obtained same day.   The reason is that punishment is deterrent and has not yet had time to have effect.

———— conviction.   Notice of, need not be given in court of R. M.   2 Juta 1, p. 2:

PRISONERS or person committed for trial to have copy of preliminary examinations on payment of 3d. per 100 words. Act 17, 1874, vol. 5, page 39, sect 11.

———— may inspect depositions, &c., without fee. *Ibid.* Sect. 12.

———— at hard labour may be fired on if necessary to prevent escape, and if such prisoner shall be killed or wounded, constable shall not be deemed guilty of any offence.   Sect. 4, Act 5, 1866–7.   Vol. 3, p. 251.

———— at hard labour.   Discipline of.   Constable may secure by binding or putting in irons any prisoner contriving or endeavouring to escape from hard labour party.   Act 5, 1866–7, vol. 3, page 251, sect. 1.   This Act applies only to hard labour party from gaol or lock-up.   10th sect. of Ordinance 24, 1847, to apply to offences while outside the precints of the gaol.   *Ibid.*   Sect. 2.

———— Escape of prisoners, or attempt to escape, conspiracy to escape, supplying any other prisoner with implements, matter or thing intended to aid in escape.   Case may be tried by R. M.   Punishment : one year's hard labour, to commence at expiration of sentence then being done, or not exceeding 50 lashes, or both imprisonment and lashes.   *Ibid.* Sect. 3.

———— of war.   Buchanan, 1879, part 2, page 45.

PRIVATE person may arrest for murder, culpable homicide, rape, robbery, or assault with intent to commit any of these crimes, or in which a dangerous wound is given.   Arson, housebreaking, theft of sheep and cattle or goat, committed in his presence.   Every arrest made on suspicion only at peril of person arresting if accused is innocent.   Ordinance 73, 1830, sects. 14–15.   Stat. Law, p. 376.

PRIVATE prosecutor under Act 27 of 1882. Any person n.ay prosecute. Act 27, 1882, sect. 22.

PRIVILEGE of legal adviser, i.e. of communication by client to. No advocate, attorney, &c., duly admitted to practice in any court of the Colony shall in any case be competent or legally compellable to give evidence *against* any person, by whom he has been professionally consulted or employed *without the consent of such person.* Matters known to any advocate, &c., before such professional employment may be disclosed. It will be observed that the privilege is that of the client and not of the lawyer. Ordinance 72, 1830, R. of C. 416.

S. L., p. 542.   ——— of creditor extended to companies and administrators.

——— in action for slander. Magistrate's words from the bench in course of any trial, are privileged, unless actual malice can be proved. 1 Juta 5, p. 319.

PRIVILEGED communication. Statement at meeting of Chamber of Commerce by a member is. 1876, part 1, page 37.

——— statement made by Town Councillor at the meeting of Council is. Buchanan, 1879, part 2, page 95.

——— witness. Not to answer when against public policy, &c., according to English Law. Ordinance 72, 1830, sect. 47 ; R. of C., page 422.

PRIVITY in contract. See " Contract," and 1879, part 1, page 16.

PROCEEDINGS. Court of R. M., page 173, sect. 7.

PROCEDURE in civil cases. Rules 14 and 15 R. of C., page 210 ; Act 20, 1856.

PROCESS of Court for summoning any person as party or witness, may be signed by clerk.

——— of Circuit Court to arrest or attach property may be issued by R. M. of district or circuit judge. Page 110, R. of C., rule 164.

PROCLAMATION of Main Roads. Governor may proclaim, alter, or revoke. Act 11, 1877, vol. 5, page 237, sect. 2.

——— Alteration. See " Closing of any divisional or other road or path." *Ibid.* Sects. 3 and 4.

PROCURATION per. Bills endorsed. See 1 Juta 1, p. 19.

PRŒDIUM rusticum and prœdium urbanum. It is not the place that creates the distinction, but the use to which that place is put. 2 Juta 1, p. 7.

PROMISSORY note or bill of exchange to be stamped. Either to be written on stamped paper or an adhesive stamp attached. Act 3, 1864, sect. 24 ; R. of C., page 301.

——— over £40 (also good for). Defendant may object to jurisdiction of R. M. in, on giving security. Act 21, 1876, sect. 3, page 289.

——— bill of exchange, &c. General issue is inadmissible, usually. Plea must traverse some matter of fact, e.g. the drawing, or making, or indorsing, or accepting, or presenting, or notice of dishonour.

——— Under the plea that defendant did not make or accept, the defence that the bill or note is lost does not arise; nor under this plea can defendant set up the alteration, unless alteration affects the stamp.

PROMISSORY note or bill of exchange. Where the bill or note is introduced as a consideration for another contract, or as a fact which, in connection with other matter, produces the cause of action, the general issue may be applicable. Thus, where an executor sued upon a promise made to himself to pay a bill due to his testator, *non-assumpsit* was held to be a proper plea.

———— signed by son as general agent per pro. Bank not required to make enquiries. Lomo's case. 1 Juta 1, page 3.

———— note. Judgment for innocent holder of note fraudulently filled up, &c., Defendant not denying signature. E. D. C. R., 2 Buchanan 2, page 108.

———— for shares. Tender of shares in summons is good. E. D. C. R., 2 Buchanan 2, page 127.

———— penalty for non-payment. Judgment refused for. E. D. C. R., 2 Buchanan 2, page 130.

———— falling due on Sundays or public holidays. See "Bills of Exchange." Act 3, 1856. Vol. 1, p. 83.

———— barred by prescription after 8 years; or any other liquid document on which provisional judgment is commonly obtained. Act 6, 1861, page 233, sect. 2.

———— holders for value. 1879, part 3, page 159.

PROOF of debts in insolvency. Every creditor must prove by affidavit. (Statute Law, page 551), or by agent's affidavit.

———— Debts not yet due. *Ibid.* Page 553, sect. 29.

———— Debts by contingent creditor. *Ibid.* Page 554, sect. 31.

PROSECUTION of all crimes, except murder, barred by lapse of 20 years. Ordinance 40, 1828. S. Law, p. 357, sect. 21.

———— of libel barred after six months. Act 46, 1882, sect. 10.

PROSECUTOR in criminal cases not appearing, Defendant may move for discharge. If prosecution be private, no private prosecutor can proceed again on same charge. Crown can take up matter if public prosecutor see fit. R. of C., page 75, Rule 74.

———— in Circuit Court. R. M. can appoint, if there be no person entitled by law to conduct such prosecution. Ordinance 8, 1852, sect. 14; R. of C., page 387.

PROTEST of any note falling due on Saturday next preceding any holiday occurring on Monday, not competent to be made until Tuesday. Act 3, 1856, sect. 3, page 84.

———— falling due on day preceding holiday, not competent to be made until day following holiday. *Ibid.* Sect. 2.

———— not necessary under £20. R. of C., page 173, sect. 7.

PROVISIONAL judgment becomes final, and security *de restituendo* becomes void at expiration of one month.

———— If provisional judgment reversed, defendant can sue on bond *de restituendo* for the recovery of sums therein mentioned. Act 20, 1856; R. of C.; rule 30, page 215.

———— Sentence refused, where alteration had been made in promissory note. Buchanan, 1875, part 2, page 84.

PROVISIONAL sentence. Obtained by default and judgment satisfied. Plaintiff ordered to go into principal case, where defendant entered appearance to defend. 1875, part 3, page 97.

———, sentence. Denial of signature. Buchanan, 1873, part 3, page 143.

——— case. Plaintiff has right of reply. Buchanan, 1876, part 2, pp. 55 and 60.

Vol. 3, p. 295.   **PUBLIC** Bodies Debts Act. Act 11, 1867.

Return of *nulla bona*. Petition to Supreme Court, &c., to levy a rate. Rule *nisi* to issue, calling on such body to show cause why relief prayed shall not be granted. *Ibid.* Sect. 1.
Rule to be served at the office of such body. *Ibid.* Sect. 2.
Rule may be made absolute if debt not satisfied, and a rate assessed not to exceed 1*d.* in the £, but second rate of 1*d.* may be assessed until debt and costs paid. Twelve months to elapse between rates. *Ibid.* Sect. 3.
Court will appoint a receiver. *Ibid.* Sect. 9.

——— Prosecutor has *right* of reply whether evidence led for defence or no. (Not used.) On prosecution instituted by crown. Page 339, Taylor, vol. 1.

PUBLICATION of names of new members of Divisional Council. When quorum elected and names published, new
Vol. 3, p. 151.   Council to come into office. Act 4, 1865, sect. 50.

PURCHASER of goods entitled in action *ex emto* to recover damages where no delivery of goods made, or where goods delivered are defective, or to have purchase price reduced to actual worth of goods sold. Buchanan, 1879, part 3, page 183.

Acts, vol. 1, p. 25.   **QUALIFICATION** for House of Assembly. Sect. 47. Constitution Ordinance.

Any person (excepting those mentioned below) entitled ˙ or qualified to be registered as a voter.

Disqualification : Any person holding office of profit under H.M. the Queen. Uncertified insolvent. Alien registered as a voter by virtue of deed of burghership.

ib. vol. 3, p. 141.   ——— for member of Divisional Council : landed proprietor, value £500. Sect. 13, Act 4, 1865. Possession of land
ib. vol. 4, p. 61.   on lease from Crown, £30 per annum. Act 3 of 1870, sect. 6.

ib. vol. 6.   **QUARANTINE** Regulation. Public Health Act, No. 4, 1883.

QUASHING, altering, amending, or reviewing conviction, by Judges. Act 20, 1856, sect. 47.

QUESTION tending to criminate. Witness may refuse to answer if not legally compellable at Westminster, by reason that questions might expose him to pains, penalties, punishment, forfeiture, or to a criminal charge, or as degrading to
R. of C., p. 422.   his character. Ordinance 72, 1830, sect. 45.

——— which if answered may tend to show that witness owes a debt, or might be exposed to a civil action, no ground for refusing to answer. *Ibid.* Sect. 46.

QUIT RENT. Apportionment of. Acts 7 of 1856 and 10 of 1875. Seller and purchaser to agree and Circuit Court to certify. Amount to be stated in transfer deed. Minimum quit rent to be 5*s*.

QUIT RENT. Action for recovery of. Certificate of Circuit Court that rent is owing shall be *prima facie* evidence of its being overdue and unpaid. Act 7, 1856, sect. 9.   Acts, vol. 1, p. 99.

—— Circuit Court to give notice to proprietor of overdue quit rents. Ordinance 9, 1844, sect. 2.   S. L., p. 684. :

—— or lease rent lands, on which the rent has not been paid for ten years, treated as derelict. If mortgaged, sects. 8, 9, 10 of Ordinance 9, 1884, to apply to scale. Act 3, 1879, sects. 1 & 2.   Acts, vol. 6.

RAILWAYS regulated by Act 19, 1861. Obstructing line, engine or carriage, so as to endanger safety of passengers. Obstruction of railway officer. Sect. 7. Travelling on, without paying fare or beyond distance paid for. Sect. 10. Offender may be brought before R. M. of district or place. Sect. 11. Malicious obstruction of railway. Sect. 15. (Would not appear to fall under ordinary jurisdiction. See "Juvenile Offenders," however.)   Acts, vol. 2, p. 253.   p. 254.   p. 256.   p. 257.   p. 258.

—— Offences committed on railway or within ten miles of line, may be dealt with by R. M. within whose district (or if line pass within ten miles of his district), just as if offence committed in the district. Act 16, 1882, sect. 2.   Vol. 6.

—— Refreshment rooms. Licences not granted by licensing board. Application made to Commission of Crown Lands.

LICENCES ON RAILWAY.

XVII. Licences for the sale of intoxicating liquors at any railway station refreshment room, upon property owned or occupied by the Government of the Colony for railway purposes, shall be granted, and shall be obtainable upon and subject to the conditions following :—

(1) The lessee or occupier may apply in writing to the Commissioner of Crown Lands and Public Works, or any officer of the railway department whom the said commissioner may appoint for that purpose, for a certificate to obtain a licence.

(2) The said commissioner or such officer may, if he sees fit, issue a certificate authorizing the grant of a retail licence by the proper stamp officer to the applicant for any period not exceeding one year to expire on the thirty-first day of March next after issue.

(3) Every licence so granted shall be renewable by the like authority for any period not exceeding one year.

(4) Any licence so granted may be transferred by the authority of the said commissioner or such officer as aforesaid.

(5) Under any such, liquors shall be sold only within a reasonable time before and after the arrival or departure of any train at a station.

(6) Any licence granted under the authority of any such certificate may at any time be cancelled by the said commissioner.

(7) For or in respect of any such licence issued for a year there shall be paid such sum as is prescribed by the said second Schedule, and for any period less than a year one-twelfth of the said sum for every month for which or the part of which the said licence is granted.

RANKING of claims in insolvent estate. Sect. 33.   S. L., p. 556.

——* of claims under fresh sequestration of creditors under former sequestration. Sect. 130.   p. 605.

---

* This refers to uncertificated insolvent and fresh sequestration under sect. 129.

S. Law, p. 605.   **RANKING** of Partnership and Companys' claims. Sect. 34.
             RAPE. Private person may arrest for. Ordinance 73, 1830, sects. 14 & 15.

S. L., pp. 559, 560.   **RECALL** of election of trustee on account of fraud. Ordinance 6, 1843, sect. 40.

Acts, vol. 3, p. 291.   **RECEIVING** stolen goods. Prisoner charged with theft before Court of R. M. may be convicted of receiving, although

p. 292.   alternative not charged. Act 9, 1867, sect. 1.
             Fine may also be imposed. Not to exceed ten times the value of the goods so stolen or received. Sect. 2. Refer also to Act 16, sect. 4.
             RECOGNIZANCE, terms of. Condition that person shall appear and answer any indictment within six months, &c.

R. of C., p. 353.   Ordinance 40, 1828, sect. 4.
             RECONVENTION. Claim in, in answer to. Plaintiff cannot set up further amount due to him, and not originally sued for. Buchanan, 1875, part 2. S. C. R., p. 44.
           ——— Plaintiff suing B, who traded as B & Co., held that B could not set off claim due to B. & Co. Buchanan, 1879, part 3, p. 165.

R. of C., p. 207.   **RECORD** of Court of R. M., how kept. Act 20 of 1856, rule 6, sched. B.
           ——— entry. Document of Court of R. M. Clerk of Court to produce without summons, or notice to produce. *Ibid.*

ib. pp. 213, 214.   Rule 23, sched. B.
p. 234.   ——— of appeal cases. Clerk of Court to forward to Court of Appeal. Rule 59.

p. 201.   ——— how kept. Persons interested or concerned may have access to. Rule 55.

Acts, vol. 6.   **REFORMATORY** Institution. Act 7, 1879.
             On conviction of child, Court may order offender to be sent to reformatory until he or she attain the age of sixteen years, or for shorter time ; or may order child to be apprenticed to useful trade up to sixteenth year. Sect. 4.
             Warrant for detention must be issued by Court, sect. 6, setting forth crime of which convicted, and period of detention, and warrant sent to reformatory. Sect. 8.
             Case to be forwarded for review under sects. 47, 48, 49, Act 20 of 1856. Sect. 25.
             REFUSAL by insolvent to be examined. Ordinance 6, 1843,

S. Law, p. 572.   sect. 64.
p. 573.   ——— by third parties (in insolvency). *Ibid.* Sect. 65.
           ——— to assist peace officer in arresting when called on.

p. 169.   Ordinance 73, 1830, sect. 13.
p. 413.   ——— penalty for so refusing. Ordinance 2, 1837, sect. 7.

R. of C., p. 132.   **REHABILITATION** of insolvent. Rules for.

Acts, vol. 3, p. 337.   **RELIGIOUS** Disabilities' Bill. Act 11 of 1868.
             REMAND. Warrant to be issued for. May be issued more than once. Reason to be specified and day of further exami-

S. Law, p. 362.   nation. Ordinance 40, 1828, sect. 36.
             REMITTAL of case under increased jurisdiction by Attorney (or Solicitor-General). Plea of guilty. Act 12 of 1860,

sect. 1. (Sects. 47, 48, 49 of Act 20, 1856, apply if sentence R. of C., p. 278.
over £5, one month, or include any lashes.)
REMOVAL of trustee in insolvent estate. Causes for; or
vacancy in office of: death of. Ordinance 6, 1843, sect. 52. S. Law. p. 566.
REMUNERATION of trustee in insolvent estate. Ordi-
nance 6, 1843, sect. 44. 5 per cent. on movable, 2½ per cent. S. Law, p. 562.
on immovable property. Buchanan, 1868, page 5. 3 Menzies S. C. R., p. 5.
268, 269. p. 252.
RENT. Action for, and return of *nulla bona.*
——— Plaintiff may summon for ejectment. Act 20, 1856,
sect. 23, rule 50, sched. B.
——— Nature or value of action must be within limits of sect.10.
——— Arrest of goods as security for. See " Arrest of Goods."
——— Removal or concealment of goods attached for rent.
with six months' imprisonment. Act 20 of 1856, sect. 31. R. of C., p. 185.
REPLY. Plaintiff has right of, except when issue of fact was
for defendant to move. Rule of Court, 131; also Rule 25, R. of C., p. 90.
Act 20, 1856. p. 214.
REPORT. Monthly, to Attorney or Solicitor-General of cases
under ordinary jurisdiction. Act 20, 1856, sect. 46. p. 193.
RESISTANCE to police may be taken under ordinary jurisdiction instead of special Act. Buchanan, 1879, part 4. S. C. R., p. 287.
——— to Police Act 27, 1882, sect. 8, part 5. Vol. 6.
RESUMPTION of action against insolvent. Ordinance 6,
1843, sect. 27. S. Law, p. 552.
RETAIL licence. Wines and spirits. Authorizes sale of
liquor in any quantity on premises specified, between 6 a.m.
and 9 p.m., excepting on Sunday, Christmas Day, Good
Friday; or such other hours as Licensing Court may fix; to be
consumed on premises or not, according to condition of licence.
Act 28, 1883. Bar must open towards the street. Sect. 9.
——— Licence holder may obtain temporary licence. (*q. v.*)
Sect. 7, Act 28, 1883—

(2) A "retail licence" shall authorize the sale of liquor in any quantity
on the premises therein specified between the hours of six in the morn-
ing and nine at night on any day other than Sunday, Christmas Day,
and Good Friday; or between such other hours as may be fixed by the
licensing court under the provisions of this Act; such liquors according
to the conditions of the licence to be consumed in or upon the seller's
house or premises, or otherwise.

(2) A " bottle licence " shall authorize the sale on the premises therein
specified, but not elsewhere, of liquors in bottles, and not to be drunk or
consumed in or upon the premises for which the licence is granted.
Under any such licence not less than one reputed quart bottle of liquor
made in the colony, nor less than one bottle of imported liquor of any
size shall be sold at one time to one person.

IX. No retail licence shall authorize the sale of liquors in any town
or village otherwise than in premises having the bar entrance opening in
or towards a public street or thoroughfare. No licence shall authorize
the sale by auction of liquors in quantities less than such as may be sold
under a wholesale licence.

REVIEW of criminal cases by judge.
——— All sentences to imprisonment over one month, all fines
above £5, and any sentence including lashes. Act 20, 1856, Acts, vol. 1, p.
sect. 47. 158.

Acts, vol. 1, p. 160.   **REVIEW.** Persons sentenced to be informed when proceedings will be sent up for review. *Ibid.* Sect. 49.

R. of C. p. 353. —— of proceedings of inferior Courts, grounds for. Ordinance 40, 1828, sect. 5.

—— Supreme Court has power of, over all inferior Courts of Justice, and can set aside or correct sentences. *Ibid.*

ib. p. 113.   Sect. 4. See also Rule 190.

RIGHT of prosecution of any crime (except murder) barred

p. 357. by lapse of twenty years. Ordinance 40, 1828, sect. 21.

—— of reply. Plaintiff has, except when defendant has to move issue of fact. See " Reply."

—— of way. Buchanan, 1876, part 2. S. C. R., p. 66.

—— Proof of custom of country before annexation necessary to claim prescription, where land has been annexed within thirty years. Buchanan, 1876, part 3, p. 165.

S. Law, pp. 895, *et seq.*   —— to water in dispute. R. M. has jurisdiction. Ordinance 5, 1848. (But not so as to bind rights in future. It is possible to assess damage done, or to impose fine for breach of contract or regulation, without overstepping this bound.)

ROAD RATES. Application of. Sects. 43, 44, 45, 46, 47, & 48, Act 9 of 1858 ; sect. 11, Act 10 of 1864.

—— Surplus. Act 9, 1858, sect. 52.

—— not payable on Crown land leased after the day on which Divisional Council has assessed its rate. Buchanan, 1876, part 1, page 48.

Acts,vol.4,p.6.   —— on Crown lands leased. Act 3 of 1870, sect. 6.

Acts, vol. 5, p. 237.   **ROADS.** Law relating to. Amended Act, 11, 1877.

—— Governor may declare main road or revoke.

—— Proclamation declaring road a main road. Act 11, 1877, sects. 2 & 3.

—— Governor may allow deviation. Divisional Council must advertise for three months.

—— Proposed deviation. Sect. 4.

—— Across property. Owner may erect swing gates. Sect. 5. Ordinance 9 of 1846 applied, except in municipalities where regulations repressing offences are already made. Sect. 6.

ROBBERY. " One of the four Crown pleas." Private person

S. Law, p. 379. may arrest for. Ordinance 73, 1830, sect. 22.

RULES of Court. Buchanan, 1875, part 4, S. C. R., p. 175 ; Buchanan, 1879, part 4, p. 295. Rule No. 10, Magistrate's Court. Proprietor of land suing. Buchanan, 1879, part 1, p. 1. Rule No. 38 (*q. v.*) is imperative. Buchanan, 1879, part 2, p. 90. Rule No. 213. Articles (of clerk to attorney) must be registered. Buchanan, 1879, part 2, p. 73.

Acts, vol. 3, p. 157.   —— and standing orders of Divisional Council. Council to frame and submit to Governor. Act 4, 1865, sect. 69.

ib.   **SALARY** of Secretary to Divisional Council. Act 4, 1865, sects. 66, 67.

Vol. 5, p. 76.   **SAVINGS** Bank. Act 4, 1875.

SCAB. Disease in Goats. Prevention of. Act 31, 1874. Penalties

p. 70. under : recoverable in Court of R. M. Sect. 7. Majority of

Divisional Council (¾th) may petition Government to put Act in force. Sect. 10.

SCIENTER in action for damages done by animal not necessary to prove. Buchanan 1876, parts 1 and 2, pp. 52, 104. Voet. 9. 1. 6. Grotius 3. 38. 13. The ordinary rule that the owner of a dog is liable for the injuries caused by his dog to another's animal, whether he knew the dog's ferocious disposition or propensity or not, must be taken with the limitation that the animal injured was lawfully at the place where it was injured. Buchanan, 1879, part 1, p. 8. See exhaustive judgment by Smith J. Buchanan, 1879, part 1, p. 29. (Appendix.)

SEAMAN. Any person purchasing stores or cargo from. Act 27, 1882, sect. 11.

SEAMEN'S ACT (Merchant). Acts 13, 1855; 3, 1863; 13, 1874; 2, 1870.   Vol. 6.

SEA PROTEST 10s. stamp. Act 13, 1870.   Acts, vol. 4. p. 93.

SEARCH Warrant on affidavit. R. M. or J. P. may grant. Ordinance 40, 1828, sect. 42.   S. Law, p. 363.

SECOND Conviction within two years. Increased punishment for. Act 20, 1856, sect. 42.   Vol. 1, p. 156.

———— Solitary confinement for. R. M. to observe regulations.   ib.

SECURITY by Secretary Divisional Council. Act 4, 1865, sect. 64.   Vol. 3, p. 156.

———— for costs of sequestration to be given. Sect. 7.   S. Law, p. 539.

———— Messenger of Court, R. M., to give to satisfaction of R. M. Act 20, 1856, rule 5.   R. of C., p. 207.

SEDUCTION. If there be a doubt, defendant is entitled to it. Buchanan, part 3.   S. C. R., p. 120.

SENTENCE of R. M. not to be reversed on account of severity (if otherwise competent). Act 20, 1856, sect. 49.   p. 160.

SEQUESTRATION. Compulsory. Sect. 5.   S. Law, p. 538.

Security to be given. Sect. 7.   p. 539.

———— of Company's estate. Sect. 9.   S. Law, p. 540.

———— of estate of persons deceased or lunatics. Sect. 10.   pp. 542, 543.

———— order of. Deposit with Sheriff, who will hand order to Master. Sect. 12.   ib.

———— may be followed out by other than the petitioning creditor. Sect. 20.   p. 546.

———— fresh : of uncertificated Insolvent. Preferent and concurrent claims will be ranked afresh of unsatisfied creditors. Sect. 130.   p. 605.

SERVANT living on premises of master to have his food unless otherwise stipulated. Act 15, 1856, sect. 9.   Acts, vol. 1, p. 110.

SERVICE of summons to be endorsed by messenger. Act 20, 1856, rule 12.

———— of summons. Number of days allowed. See "Induciæ." Act 20, 1856, rule 10.   p. 209.

———— of summons. Copy of deed of transfer need not accompany. Buchanan, 1879, part 1, page 1.

———— of summons on any officer of bank within usual banking hours, under Bank Note Act, is good service. Act 6, 1875, sect. 6.   Acts, vol. 5, p. 81.

SERVICE of Subpœna and penalties for non-attendance. Act 20, 1856, rules 18 & 75.

SET OFF. Taxed costs of application for civil imprisonment in a case where applicant was unsuccessful, are a set off against original debt, and not a cause for dismissing fresh application. Supreme Court, 1 Juta 5, page 358. See " Civil Imprisonment Court of R. M." Costs of an application of this nature are borne by applicant, unless defendant's conduct be shown to be vexatious.

SETTING dog to worry or attack any person or animal. Damage done to cattle. Act 27, 1882, sect. 7, par 9. See "Dog" also, and "Scienter."

SHEEPKILLING. No such *crime* known to our law. Buchanan, 1876, part 1, page 53.

SHEPHERD. Failure to preserve portions of goat that died. See "Masters and Servants."

SHERIFF Deputies, and Messenger, Court R. M., serve order for compulsory sequestration fees. Ordinance 6, 1843, sect. 16.

S. Law, p. 544.

———— or Messenger, officer of customs selling wines, spirituous liquors in executions of his officer does come under Act 28, 1883, sect. 5.

Acts, vol. 1, p. 38.

SHIPS Stores from Bond, not liable to duty. Foreign going vessel. Act 8, 1855.

Vol. 1, p. 53.

SHIPPING Act. Merchant Seaman's. Act 13, 1855. Amended by Act 13, 1874.

Vol. 5, p. 12.

SHOP Retail. Ordinance 11, 1846.

SHORT Service of indictment. Prisoner and prosecutor consenting, prisoner may be brought to trial at any time after commitment for trial. Ordinance 40, 1828, sect. 60.

R. of C., p. 369.

———— Service. Prisoner electing to proceed to trial covers defect (condones short service). Rule of Court No. 72, 1879 ; Buchanan, part 2, page 105.

S. C. R., p. 105.
S. L., p. 82.

SILVER a legal tender in this Colony. Ordinance 2, 1825.

SKINS. Theft of. Provisions of Cattle Theft Repression Act, extended to. Act 17, 1874, sect. 1, page 405. Tennant's Rules. Act 17, 1867, also extended to crime of "attempting" to steal any animal or skin.

SLANDER. Defendant acting *bona fide* and without malice, words not actionable. 1879, part 2, page 95.

———— Privilege—Magistrates' words from the bench are privileged, unless he be actuated by malice, which will not be lightly assumed. 1 Juta 5, p. 319.

SLAUGHTERING or skinning any animal or beast in a public thoroughfare. Act 27, 1882, sect 7, part 8.

SOUND and Sober Senses. Magistrate to satisfy himself that prisoner is in ; before proceeding against him continue. Ordinance 40, 1828, sect. 33.

S. Law, p. 361.

SPECIAL constable can be appointed by J. P. to convey prisoner to gaol—and shall be paid for service as if appointed by Field Cornet. Ordinance 9, 1848. Act 10, 1876, sect. 8. R. of C., page 285.

Vol. 5, p. 165.

———— Justices of the Peace. Act 10, 1876.

SPECIFIC performance of contract. Defendant allowed to pay damages in contract of sale of landed property. Buchanan, 1879, part 3, page 155.

—— performance. Where in action on a lease plaintiff failed to obtain order for—damages not allowed. Buchanan, 1879, part 4, page 233.

SQUATTING on municipal land is not an "offence under Vagrancy Act. E. D. C. R., 2 Buchanan 2, p. 157.

STALLION or Jackass. Trespass. Sect. 51. Ordinance 16, 1847, page 846.

STAMP. Contract not stamped according to *lex loci contractus*, admissible if stamped according to Stamp Acts. 1 Juta 1, page 1.

STAMPS. Documents that ought to be stamped, but are un-stamped, admissible in criminal cases in spite of omission. Vol. 5, p. 38, sect. 8.

—— fees collected by means of Stamps, see " Fees." Vol. 5, p. 246.

—— examination of stock of. Act 3, 1864, sect. 9, page 295.

—— Postage—to be used for postage only. Act 1, 1868. Vol. 3, p. 327.

—— and licenses act of. Act 3, 1864; Act 10, 1869; 13, 1870; 11, 1871; 14, 1873.

STATIONER'S assistant. Not a Servant under Masters and Servants Act. 1879, part 1, page 22.

STOP, search, and detain any vessel, boat, cart, &c., &c., suspected of having stolen goods, and any person on reasonable grounds of suspicion—by private person—if person would probably escape, if not arrested. Act 27, 1882, sect. 18.

STREET or road, &c. Encumbering and causing damage to. *Ibid.* Sect. 7.

SUB-LETTING. See "Ejectment for breach of contract or condition."

SUBPOENA to produce document. Act 20, 1856, pages 211 and 212, rule 17.

—— for witness, in civil cases. *Ibid.* Page 211, rule 16.

SUBSTITUTION, power of—in assigned estate. 1876, part 2, page 88.

SUCCESSION Act. Act 23, 1874.

SUITS for or against Divisional Council. Act 4, 1865, vol. 3, page 157, sect. 71.

SUMMONS to witnesses to be issued by Clerk of the Court. Act 20, 1856, rule 16, page 211. R. of C.

—— by clerk to R. M. Ordinance 8, 1852. S. Law, p. 980.

—— of insolvent for adjudication of sequestration. Sect. 17. S. Law, p. 545.

—— how served—in absence of insolvent. *Ibid.*

—— Main object of—to bring defendant into Court. Buchanan, 1876, part 3, page 125.

SUNDAY. No service of civil process on—except arrest (rule also applies to holiday). It would seem, therefore, that a debtor can be arrested for debt on a Sunday or a holiday. R. of C., page 43, rule 10. Supreme C. rules.

SURPLUS of road rates, how expended. Act 9, 1858, sect. 52.

F

SURRENDER of estate. Petition to Supreme Court. Statute Law, page 536.

—— of insolvent. Proceedings of Supreme Court. Tennant's Rules, page 136.

SURVEY, Expenses of. Act 10, 1874.

TACIT Hypothec. Act 5, 1861.

Vol. 5, p. 126. **TAME** ostriches. See "Ostriches." Act 24, 1875.

TAXATION of costs in Periodical Court, by person appointed to issue process, but under supervision and control of R. M., who shall sign or initial the bill of costs. Act 9, 1857, sect. 8, page 275, R. of C.

TAXES municipal—Government property free from. Ordinance 3, 1843.

TELEGRAPHIC messages protected. Act 8, 1880.

TELEGRAPHS. Act 20, 1861, and 5, 1862.

TEMPORARY Licence. Sum to be fixed by R. M., not to exceed 10s. per diem. Schedule to Act 28, 1883.

TEMPORARY LICENCES.

XVIII. Any person being the holder of a retail licence may apply to the resident magistrate for a certificate authorizing the distributor of stamps to issue a temporary licence for the sale of liquors at any place of recreation or amusement.

XIX. The resident magistrate to whom any such application shall be made may, if he shall see fit, grant a certificate wherein shall be stated the name of the applicant, the place where such temporary licence is to be granted, the number of days during which sales are authorized, and such restrictions and conditions as such magistrate may impose: time mentioned in any such certificate may be extended, but the licence shall not endure for longer than eight days in all,

(4) A " temporary licence" shall authorize the dealer, being also the holder of a retail licence, to sell liquors by retail at any place of recreation or public amusement for the period stated therein, subject to such restrictions and conditions as the resident magistrate authorizing the issue of the same shall think fit.

TENDER of expenses to third persons to be examined in insolvent estate. Ordinance 6, 1843, sect. 66.

S. Law, p. 573.

—— If defendant after tender relies on legal defence, he cannot on failure of defence rely on tender to save costs. Buchanan, 1875, part 1, page 23.

—— plea of, cannot be pleaded together with general issue to same cause of action. Buchanan, 1875, part 2, page 38.

—— plea of, following plea of general issue does not relieve from costs on judgment being recovered for amount of tender made. Buchanan, 1875, part 2, page 40.

—— if excepted to, as bad and insufficient, can be withdrawn.

TENURE of office of Divisional Council, triennial. Act 4, 1865, sect. 57.

Vol. 3, p. 155.

THEFT is a continuous crime, so long as property is in possession of the thief.

THEFT on indictment for, in Court of R. M. prisoner may be convicted of receiving stolen goods, if evidence be sufficient to substantiate such alternative finding, as if indictment had been specially framed for the crime of "Receiving." Act 9, 1867, sect. 1.   Vol. 3, p. 291.

THEFT. Person convicted may also be fined any amount not exceeding ten times the value of the article stolen or received. *Ibid.* Sect. 2.   p. 292.

—— of cattle—sheep or goat—private person may arrest. Ordinance 73, 1830, sects. 14, 15.   S. Law, p. 376.

—— Magistrate may assess value of stolen cattle and give judgment for. Act 16, 1864.

—— Magistrate to have jurisdiction in theft of cattle, sheep or goats. (See "Skins," *ante.*)

Punishment: One year imprisonment; or imprisonment with or without spare diet, three months; or, twenty-five lashes for first conviction, thirty-six lashes second conviction. Proof of second conviction must be within three years. Act 17, 1867, vol. 3, page 313.

—— Provisions of sects. 43, 47, 48, & 49, of Act 20, 1856, applies, whatever the imprisonment inflicted and whatever number of lashes ordered. Act 17, 1867, sect. 4.   Vol. 3, p. 314.

—— Preliminary examination to be taken, when R. M. shall consider case unfit to be disposed of under limited Jurisdiction Act. *Ibid.* Sect. 6.

Plea of guilty. Case remitted to R. M. Act 18, 1879.

Plea of *not* guilty and case remitted, penalties provided under this Act may be ordered on conviction.

Proceedings may be converted into preliminary examination by R. M. Act 17, 1867, vol. 3, page 314, sect. 7.

Act to apply to crime of receiving stolen cattle with guilty knowledge. *Ibid.* Page 315, sect. 8.

Or receiving any portion of the carcase or the carcase of any animal. Act 18, 1879.

Attorney-General may remit for theft if prisoner committed for receiving, and for receiving if prisoner committed for theft. Act 17, 1867, sect. 9.   Vol. 3, p. 316.

Definition of the word *Cattle.* Shall mean any horse, mare, gelding, colt or filly, mule or ass, or any bull, cow, ox, heifer, or calf. *Ibid.* Sect. 10.

—— Magistrate may give judgment for value of cattle on summary conviction. Act 21, 1876, sect. 6.   Vol. 5, p. 186.

—— of the use. (*Furtum usus.*) By Mr. Justice Smith, if a man take another's horse without his permission, merely for a ride, he does not commit the crime of theft. 2 Juta 1, p. 44.

—— of the *use* of a boat, punishable by Act 27, 1882, sect. 12.   Vol. 6, p. 478.

—— Two persons claiming property. One takes possession. This does not constitute theft. E. D. C. R., 2 Buchanan 2, page 158.

THOROUGHFARE, obstructing by leaving timber, plough, &c., penalized. Act 27, 1882, sect. 7, parts 4 & 6.   Vol. 6, p. 476.

TOLLS and toll bars on main roads, sects. 14, 15, 16, 17, 18, of Act 9, 1858, and sect. 5, of Act 10, 1864.

—— schedule regulating, on main roads. Act 22, 1873, page 303.

TOLLS and toll bars on divisional roads. Sects. 22 & 23, Act 9, 1858, and sect. 6, Act 10, 1864.

———— on ferries, the property of Divisional Councils. Act 10,

Vol. 3, p. 43.   1864, sects. 4, 5, 6, 7.

———— bars, *erection* of, by Divisional Council within *municipal limits*. Repugnant portions of Act 9 of 1858, and 10 of 1864, repealed. Act 7, 1869.

Divisional Council must obtain consent of municipality to erect tollbars within limits, and may agree to pay portion of

Vol. 4, p. 15.   toll money levied to municipality. Sect. 2.

Existing tollbars not to be interfered with. *Ibid.* Sect. 3.

Vol. 4, p. 256.   ———— on *traction engines*, regulated. Act 6, 1873.

Traction engine four times the toll of wagon with same number of wheels. *Ibid.* Sect. 1.

wagons drawn by traction engine, *ordinary toll*. *Ibid.* Sect. 2.

TORT or wrong. In action for—General issue operates as a denial of the breach of duty only, or wrongful act committed by defendant, and not of the facts stated in the "inducement" (i.e. that part of the declaration or summons, which contains a statement of the facts out of which the charge arises, or which are necessary or useful to make the charge intelligible), and no other defence than such denial shall be admissible under this plea; all other pleas in denial shall take issue on some particular matter of fact alleged in the declaration, e.g.—

In an action for a nuisance to the occupation of a house by carrying on an offensive trade, the plea of general issue will operate only as a denial that defendant carried on alleged trade in such a way as to be a nuisance to the occupation of the house, and not as a denial of plaintiff's occupation of the house.

Right of way, as a denial of the obstruction, not of plaintiff's right of way.

Libel, defamation, or slander of plaintiff in his office, profession, or trade, plea of general issue will operate as a denial of speaking the words, of speaking them maliciously and with reference to plaintiff's office, profession, or trade, but not as a denial of plaintiff holding that office, being of that trade, &c.

Loss of goods by carrier, as denial of loss or damage, but not of receipt of goods as a carrier for hire, or for the purpose for which received.

Damage caused by unskilful driving. Plea of general issue admits defendant to be the driver and horse and cart his, or that his servants were the persons in charge, and merely puts in issue the fact of negligence or mismanagement.

Malicious prosecution. General issue traverses the fact of prosecution, malice, probable cause.

"Dog," puts in issue the "Scienter" and the dogs propensity. See "Scienter."

"Nuisance." Under general issue plaintiff must prove that there was a nuisance, and that it was caused by defendant.

"Libel or slander." Privilege need not be specially pleaded.

"Warranty." General plea puts in issue both warranty and unsoundness, while admitting sale or bargain (perhaps, plaintiff will probably have to prove the sale, as without a sale there would be no deceit, which is the root of the matter).

Negligence, contributory. — Defendant may show plaintiff's—under general issue, but such negligence must be the immediate cause of the damage.

"Trespass." General issue admits plaintiff's possession, but denies defendant committed a trespass in the place alleged. Denial of possession must be specially pleaded.

" Unlawfully detaining goods and converting them to one's use." General issue denies " conversion" or wrongful act, but not plaintiff's title.

"Assault." General issue, merely denies. Defendant may show that plaintiff ran or drove against him, or that his horse was rendered *ungovernable* by the act of God or of a third person or superior agency, but cannot prove under the plea, that it was unintentional or merely accidental.

" False imprisonment." Judge may justify under general plea. A Resident Magistrate must plead *specially*.

" Trespass." Declaration must give *locus in quo*, " not guilty," by statute. Person entitled to plead may give evidence of special matter under—Court will not in general allow special plea. General plea should set forth particular statute and office under which defendant pleads. But the text-books are doubtful on this point. But see Ordinance 32 of 1827, sects. 5, 6, 7, 8, 9, 10, 11.

If plaintiff prove, he can recover damage without proving special damage. 1 Juta 4, p. 276.

TRADE beyond boundaries of the Colony: Ordinance 81, 1830.

TRADEMARKS, imitation of. Act 12, 1864.   Vol. 3, p. 55
Forfeiture of goods for imitation of. *Ibid.* Sect. 2.
Forging, or applying to any article. *Ibid.* Sect. 3.
Selling article with forged trademark, fine of value of article sold and penalty not exceeding £5 and not less than 10s. *Ibid.* Sect. 4.
R. M. can summon witnesses to give information. Penalty for refusing, £5. *Ibid.* Sect. 6.
Limitation of prosecution 3 years, or one year after prosecutor shall discover. *Ibid.* Sect. 18.

TRADESMEN engaged by week, unless otherwise agreed, Vol. 1, p. 109. service to terminate on Saturday. Act 15, 1856, sect. 2.

TRANSFER dues. A contract made whereby defendant obtained full rights over property. Held, by a majority, that Government was not entitled to payment of dues. (Sir J. H. de Villiers diss.) Reversed on appeal.

TRANSFER dues. Ordinance 18, 1844, Act 15, 1855, Act 7, 1858, Act 8, 1861, 11 of 1863, 7 of 1864, 4 of 1872.

TRANSFER, fines on non-payment of, after six months

Vol. 5, p. 199.   12 per cent. interest to be charged.   Act 3, 1877, sect. 2.

—— and auction dues.   Duties of Treasurer-General extended to R. M.   Ordinance 13, 1844, sect. 2.   C. C. Capetown.

R. M. to accept autioneer's security and grant certificate. Vol. 5, page 148, sect. 3.

Recognizance under sect. 8 of Ordinance 6, 1844, to be entered into before C. C. or R. M.   *Ibid.*   Sect. 4.

Transfer dues to be collected by C. C.   *Ibid.*   Sect. 5.

TRAVELLING expenses of members of Divisional Council, not to exceed 10s. per diem only if resident fifteen miles from

Vol. 4, p. 24.   place of meeting.   Act 15, 1869, sect. 3.

TREES, planting and cultivation of, encouraged.   Act 4, 1876, vol. 5, page 149.

Divisional Council or municipality may expend funds to, or offer rewards for.   *Ibid.*   Sect. 1.

Account to be kept and sent to Commissioner of Crown Lands.   *Ibid.*   Sect. 2.

Governor may return one half, not to exceed £250 in any one year, to Divisional Council of municipality.   *Ibid.* Sect. 3.

TRESPASS and pound regulations.   Ordinance 16, 1847, Act 1, 1869, 31, 1875.

—— in any place and refusing to leave, when warned by owner or occupier of such place, to do so.   Act 27, 1882, sect. 7, part 12.

—— Exception of non-joinder of owner disallowed.   1875, part 4, page 136.

—— Infringement of right of way can be tried in form of action for, 1875, part 4, page 141.

TRIAL by Jury.   Grand jurors summoned.   Buchanan, 1876, part 2, page 84.

—— in civil cases.   Procedure to have new trial.   Buchanan, 1879, part 3, page 156.

TRUSTEE in insolvency, elected at 2nd meeting, except when

S. Law, p. 549.   value under £75.

p. 559.   —— Election of, not to exceed *three* in number. *Ibid.* Sect. 40.

—— elected by votes of greater part in number and value of creditors and agents are entitled to vote.   Appeal allowed. *Ibid.*

—— provisionally appointed by Court until creditor's choose.

p. 561.   *Ibid.*   Sect. 43.

—— in insolvent estate.   Powers of trustee provisionally

S. Law, p. 561.   appointed, before creditors choose.   Sect. 43.

p. 652.   —— remuneration of.   *Ibid.*   Sect. 44.

—— to elect as to action for or against estate, or as to bring-

p. 566.   ing action.   *Ibid.*   Sect. 50.

p. 567.   —— dead, does not affect his acts.   *Ibid.*   Sect. 53.

—— nor abate actions pending.   *Ibid.*   Sect. 54.

p. 568.   —— to call meetings of creditors.   *Ibid.*   Sect. 56.

TUTORS.   Curators, &c.   Act 14, 1864.

UNDEFENDED Case. Action for delivery of Policies of Assurance. Evidence should be led for plaintiff in. Buchanan, 1879, part 3, page 152.

UNDISCHARGED Insolvent. Creditor may apply for compulsory sequestration on new debts by Ordinance 6, 1843, sect. 129. St. Law, p. 605.

UNSTAMPED Documents. Penalty on. See "Penalty," Act 3, 1864, sect. 14, pages 297, 298.

——— tendered in Evidence. R. M. may direct stamps not exceeding five times ordinary value to be affixed and document then becomes valid. Act 16, 1877, sect. 7. Vol. 5, p. 247.

——— instruments liable to Stamp Duty are admissible in evidence in criminal cases. Act 17, 1874, sect. 8, page 407.

VACATION of Supreme Court. During, one judge to be competent to execute all powers, jurisdiction, and authority of Court. Act 23, 1875, sect. 1. Vol. 5, p. 126.

——— of Seat as member of Divisional Council. Act 4, 1865, sect. 58. Vol. 3, p. 155.

——— of Divisional Council to be triennially. *Ibid.* Sect. 57.

VACCINATED. All persons appointed to Public Service to be. Sect. 60, Act. 4, 1883.

VAGRANCY and Squatting Prevention Act. Act 23, 1879.

——— Act. Lawful excuse for presence on private property. The judges held, that prisoner's excuse, that he went to see his friend, the complainant's shepherd, was a lawful excuse. Buchanan, 1879, part 4, page 214.

——— Act. Magistrate ordering prisoner to go to work must fix rate of wages. 1 Juta 3, p. 239.

——— Women employed occasionally as laundresses, &c., are not vagrants. E. D. C. R., 2 Buchanan 4, p. 386.

VALUATION for Divisional Council Purposes. Act No. 9, 1858, sects. 27, 28, 34, 35, and 37; Act No. 10, 1864, sect. 38; and the whole of Act 5, 1860.

VALUATOR'S Court and Oath of. See "Oath," Act 10, 1864, sect. 36. Vol. 3, p. 51.

VALUE of Insolvent's Estate under £75. Debts ranked and Trustee elected at *first* meeting. S. Law, pp. 549, 550.

VEHICLE. Driver going wrong side and causing injury thereby. Act 27, 1882, sect. 7, part 1.

Driver leaving his cattle so as to lose full control of them. *Ibid.* Part 2.

Driver (or rider) not keeping proper side or not permitting to pass. *Ibid.* Part 3.

VESTING of property. Divisional Council. Act 9, 1858, sect. 58.

——— of Insolvent's rights in Master of Supreme Court for purpose of Sequestration. Insolvent cannot alienate property, nor can property be attached. Statute Law, page 562, sect. 46.

——— in Trustee or in provisional Trustee. *Ibid.* Page 563, sects. 47 and 48.

VESTING of estate during vacancy in office of Trustee in Master of Supreme Court. *Ibid.* Page 567, sect. 53.

────── of estate in Trustee newly appointed. *Ibid.*

S. Law, p. 546.　**VEXATIOUS** or malicious petition. Sect. 19.

VILLAGES' Management Act. Act 29, 1881.

Amended by Act 28, 1882, so as to allow them to obtain police.

VINE Cuttings. Diseased. Importation of such articles may be prohibited by Proclamation of Governor. Act 9, 1876, vol. 5, page 163, sect. 1.

Governor may fix penalty for importing. *Ibid.* Sect. 2.

R. M. may inspect. Penalty if obstructed not exceeding £50, or six months' hard labour. *Ibid.* Sect. 3.

R. M. or Custom Officer may destroy if found to be diseased. *Ibid.* Sect. 4. See also Act 27, 1880.

VOLUNTARY surrender of estate by insolvent. Statute Law, pages 536, 537.

VOLUNTEER Corps. Formation of. Act 10, 1878. *Repealed.* Act 10, 1882.

VOTES of creditors in insolvent estate. How reckoned as to number and value. No creditor under £30 to reckon in

S. Law, p. 559.　number. Ordinance 6, 1843, sect. 38.

────── of creditors by agent. What votes determine. *Ibid.* Sect. 39.

pp. 553, 554.　**VOTING** by creditors holding security or lien. *Ibid.* Sect. 30.

p. 543.　────── by company or administrators. *Ibid.*

WANDERING abroad without visible lawful means of support, &c. Act 23, 1879, sect. 2. .

WANTONLY ringing any public bell, creating a noise or disturbance, or throwing stones. Act 27, 1882, sect. 5, part 2.

WARD. Crime against. Guardian may prosecute for.

S. Law, p. 356.　Ordinance 40, 1828, sect. 16. See also sect. 51, Act 20, 1856, in case of refusal.

────── elections. Divisional Council. Number elected for more than one ward. Act 4, 1865, sect. 48.

WARNING or notice to be given by master or servant one month, if monthly, or one week if a weekly servant, unless stipulated that notice unnecessary. Act 15, 1856, chap. 2,

Vol. 1, p. 110.　sect. 7.

────── if not acted upon, considered withdrawn. *Ibid.* Sect. 8. Wages may be fixed by R. M.

WARRANT of apprehension must be issued by J. P. before whom information on oath taken. It may be to bring person before R. M. of Division or any other J. P. specified therein. See *Renck* v. *Orsthingus*, 1 Juta 99. See application, *Fennell & Shaw* v. *Basque J. P.* E. D. Court.

WARRANT of apprehension. May be issued on information on oath by chief or other judge, R. M., J. P. R. M. or J. P. to grant warrant only, when offence has been committed within his jurisdiction, or when the person accused is within the limits of his jurisdiction and on written application. Ordinance 73, 1830, sect. 9 ; R. of C., page 374.

———— for further examination. More than once if necessary. Cause of remand shall be expressed and warrant shall specify date of further examination. Ordinance 40, 1828, sect. 36. R. of C.

S. Law, p. 362.

———— of committal to express clearly the crime or offence charged. *Ibid.* Sect. 35.

———— of commitment for trial must precede right of admission to bail. R. M. may use his own discretion. *Ibid.* Sect. 37.

———— of commitment of insolvent to specify questions asked and refused. Sect. 68.

S. Law, p. 574.

———— of removal. Magistrate may sign for removal of prisoner from one gaol to another. Ordinance 73, 1830, sect. 22, page 379.

———— of liberation. Attorney-General may grant. Ordinance 40, 1828, sect. 10, page 354.

WARRANTY. General issue operates only as denial of sale and warranty, not as denial of breach of warranty.

WASHING in, defiling or polluting public stream or water. Act 27, 1882, sect. 5, part 1.

WASTE lands. No land situate within any municipal limits to be treated as. Act 14, 1878. Sect. 13.

Vol. 5, p. 84.

WATER. Conveyance over land of other persons of. Act 26, 1882. (Act 24, 1876, repealed.)

———— rights of upper proprietor to water, *ernufpactum in suo.* 1876, part 1, page 18, also page 25.

———— of lower proprietor. 1879, part 2, page 79.

———— rights. Court of R. M. has jurisdiction in all complaints and disputes arising within their respective districts.

Wrongful division or appropriation. Ordinance 5, 1848.

Stat. Law, pp. 896–7.

There are of course many limitations to this jurisdiction. It would probably be better for the R. M. invariably, unless both parties consent to jurisdiction, to inquire first into the question as to binding future rights of proprietors.

WEARING apparel, bedding, tools of trade, £5 in whole, exempt from attachment. Rule 15, page 177, Act 20, 1856.

WEEDS. Extirpation of. Chairman Divisional Council. Act 27, 1864.

WEIGHTS and Measures. Regulation of. Act 11, 1858.

Vol. 1, p. 317.

Penalty if weight or measure be faulty. Seizure and fine not exceeding £5. *Ibid.* Sect. 10.

p. 321.

Penalty for obstructing visiting officer, refusal to produce weights, &c. Forfeiture of faulty weights, steelyards, &c., and fine not exceeding £5. *Ibid.* Sect. 11.

Powers transferred to municipalities, &c. Act 15, 1876.

Vol. 5, p. 177.

WHIPPING. In no case to be inflicted until proceedings returned with judge's certificate. Act 17, 1874, sect. 6, vol. 4, page 38 ; and Act 21, 1876, sect. 5.

Vol. 5, p. 186.

WHOLESALE Licence for wines and spirits. Sect. 6, Act 28, 1883.

WHOLESALE LICENCES.

XI. No Certificate from a licensing court shall be required in respect of the granting of the following licences:—
A wholesale licence for the sale of liquors in any municipality, or in any town or village which is the seat of a court of resident magistrate: or a licence for the sale of liquors at any railway refreshment room : or a temporary licence : or a club licence.

XII. Any person may upon application to the stamp distributor of stamps obtain a wholesale licence for the sale of intoxicating liquors within the limits prescribed for any municipality, or within the limits of any town or village which shall be the seat of a court of resident magistrate; and for the purposes of this section the limits of any such town or village, not being a municipality, shall if defined for the purposes of the "Villages Management Act, 1881," be such limits, and if not so defined, shall be deemed to be a circle of two miles in diameter, having the court-room of the resident magistrate's court for its centre.

XIII. No wholesale licence for the sale of liquors beyond the limits of any municipality or of any town or village as in the last preceding section defined, shall be granted except upon the certificate of a licensing court, as in this Act provided.

XIV. Wholesale licences may be issued in the name of a company or co-partnership where two or more persons carry on business as a company or co-partnership in the same house or premises.

XV. Any person holding a wholesale licence may store any liquors in any number of stores or places approved of by the resident magistrate and described in or endorsed upon the licence, but no one of such stores or places shall be distant from any such stores or places more than two miles.

   (1) A "wholesale licence" shall authorize a dealer to sell and deliver liquors in quantities of not less than five gallons if in cask, or one unbroken case containing not less than twelve reputed quart, or twenty-four reputed pint, bottles, to be delivered at one time, such liquor not to be consumed in or upon the seller's premises.

AN ACT TO AMEND AND CONSOLIDATE THE LAWS REGULATING THE SALE OF INTOXICATING LIQUORS.—[Assented to 27th September, 1883.]

Whereas it is expedient to amend and consolidate the laws regulating the sale of intoxicating liquors: Be it enacted by the Governor of the Cape of Good Hope, with the advice and consent of the Legislative Council and House of Assembly thereof, as follows:

I. The laws mentioned in the first schedule to this Act, to the extent to which the same are therein expressed to be repealed, shall be and the same are hereby repealed except as to offences committed against, or proceedings commenced or pending under any of such repealed laws, and except as to subsisting licences which shall, during the interval between the coming into operation of this Act and the expiration of such licences respectively, be deemed and judged of in respect of the sales and dealings which they shall be held to authorize, and the liabilities which the holders thereof shall incur, as if the said repealed laws still remained in force.

—— Liquor Licensing Act, 1883, does not apply to auctioneer selling for licensed dealer on licensed premises, or for wine farmer in quantities not less than 7 gallons, as in sub-section 3.

"LIQUOR LICENSING ACT, 1883."

GOVERNMENT NOTICE.—No. 143, 1884.

Colonial Secretary's Office,
Cape Town, Cape of Good Hope,
7th February, 1884.

Public attention is specially invited to the subjoined provisions of the above Act.

THOMAS C. SCANLAN,
Colonial Secretary.

EXTRACTS:—*Liquor Licensing Act, No. 28 of* 1883.

OFFENCES AND PENALTIES.

Offences by licensed persons which render the holder of a licence liable to a penalty not exceeding ten pounds for first and forty pounds for any subsequent conviction.

LXXIII. The holder of any licence who shall be guilty of any of the following acts or offences shall upon conviction be liable in respect of each act or offence to a penalty not exceeding ten pounds; that is to say, if he shall

(1) Permit drunkenness, or any violent, riotous or quarrelsome conduct to take place upon his premises.

(2) Sell liquor to any person already in a state of intoxication or by any means encourage or incite any person to drink liquor.

(3) Knowingly harbour or suffer to remain on his premises any constable or policeman during any time appointed for such constable to be upon duty unless for the purpose of keeping or restoring order, or in the execution of his duty.

(4) Suffer any unlawful game or gambling to be carried on on his premises.

(5) Permit his premises to be a brothel, or the habitual resort or place of meeting of reputed prostitutes.

(6) Sell or knowingly permit to be sold to any person apparently under the age of fifteen years, any description of spirits, or permit or suffer any such person to drink any such spirits upon his premises.

(7) Keep his licensed premises open for the sale of liquor, or sell or expose any liquor for sale, during any time when he is not authorized by the licence to sell, or allow any liquors purchased before the hour of closing to be consumed on such premises.

And in the case of a second or subsequent conviction every such holder shall be liable to a penalty not exceeding forty pounds.

Offences regarding the adulteration of liquor, and sale of adulterated liquor, which render any person on conviction liable to a penalty not exceeding twenty pounds.

LXXIV. Every person who shall be guilty of any of the following acts or offences shall upon conviction be liable in respect of each act or offence to a penalty not exceeding twenty pounds : that is to say, if he shall

(1) Wilfully mix or cause to be mixed with any liquors any injurious, poisonous, or deleterious ingredient or material to adulterate the same for sale.

(2) Sell, or keep or offer for sale any liquor with which any ingredient or material injurious to the health of persons drinking such liquor has been mixed.

Penalties for dealing in liquors without a licence.

LXXV. Any person who shall contrary to the provisions of this Act sell, deal in or dispose of intoxicating liquors without a licence, or sell or offer, or expose for sale any such liquors at any place where he is not

76   ALPHABETICAL COMMON PLACE BOOK.

authorized by his licence to sell the same, shall upon conviction be liable
to the following penalties, that is to say :

For the first offence a penalty not exceeding twenty-five pounds, and
in default of payment being made or security given for the
same, to imprisonment with or without hard labour for any
period not exceeding three months unless such penalty be
sooner paid or levied.

For a second offence a penalty not exceeding fifty pounds, and in
default of payment or security as aforesaid being made or given,
to imprisonment with or without hard labour for any period not
exceeding six months, unless such penalty be sooner paid or
levied.

For a third or any subsequent offence a penalty not exceeding one
hundred pounds, and in default of payment or security as aforesaid being made or given, to imprisonment with or without hard
labour for any period not exceeding twelve months, unless
such penalty be sooner paid or levied ; or to both such penalty
and such imprisonment.

In addition to any other penalty imposed by this section, the convict-
ing magistrate or special justice of the peace, as the case may be, may in
case of a second or subsequent conviction of any person for any offence in
this section mentioned, within three years previously, adjudge that such
person shall, if he be the holder of a licence under this Act, or the holder
of a retail shop licence, forfeit such licence, or both such licences if both
be held by such person, and that the offender be disqualified from taking
out any other retail shop licence during the remainder of the then current
year, and also from holding any licence for the sale of intoxicating liquors
for any term of years or at any time.

*Offences which render the holder of any retail licence or bottle licence
liable to forfeiture thereof.*

LXXVI. The holder of any retail licence or bottle licence shall be
liable to forfeit such licence

(1) If he shall permit any other person to manage, superintend, or
conduct the business of the licensed premises during his absence
for a longer period than one month without the consent, in
writing, of the resident magistrate.

(2) If he shall, whether present in such premises or not, permit any
unlicensed person to be in effect the owner of the business of
the licensed premises, unless with the consent of the licensing
court.

(3) If (being the keeper of any inn or hotel) he shall fail to provide
and maintain the accommodation required according to the
conditions prescribed by the licensing court granting such
licence.

(4) If (except in the case of fire, tempest, or other cause beyond his
control) he shall allow the licensed premises to become ruinous
or dilapidated.

(5) If he shall permit his premises to be a brothel, or if he shall sell
liquor to any person already in a state of intoxication.

(6) If he shall be twice convicted of selling, offering or keeping for
sale any adulterated liquor.

(7) If he shall be convicted of any offence under this Act, and a
previous conviction within the preceding six months of the same
or any other offence under this Act shall be proved.

(8) If he shall be convicted of any crime and sentenced to imprisonment without the option of a fine.

*Penalty on persons convicted of making false representations for the
purpose of obtaining liquor.*

LXXX. Every person who, by falsely representing himself to be a
traveller or a lodger, buys or obtains, or attempts to buy or obtain at any
premises any liquor during the period for which such premises are to be

closed under this Act or otherwise, shall upon conviction be liable to a penalty not exceeding five pounds.

Circumstances under which a resident magistrate may forbid sale of liquor by licensed persons to certain individuals under a penalty of not exceeding five pounds.

LXXXIX. The resident magistrate of any district may by an order in writing, forbid the selling of liquor to any person who

Shall within the space of three months have been thrice convicted of drunkenness, or, who having been twice so convicted shall also have been convicted of assault;—or

By excessive drinking of liquor misspends, wastes, or lessens his estate, or greatly impairs his health, or endangers the peace of his family.

Every such order shall be in force during such time as the said magistrate may determine, not however exceeding twelve months, in the district wherein the same was granted and in any other district into which such person may remove or be. Every licensed person who shall with a knowledge of such prohibition sell to any such person any liquor, and every other person who with such knowledge shall give to, purchase or procure for such prohibited person any liquor shall on conviction be liable to a penalty not exceeding five pounds, in respect of each offence.

Proof of consumption of liquor sufficient to prove sale.

LXXVII. In any proceeding relative to any offence under this Act it shall not be necessary to show that any money actually passed, or that any liquor was actually consumed, if the court hearing the case be satisfied that a transaction in the nature of a sale actually took place, or that any consumption of liquor was about to take place; and proof of consumption, or intended consumption of liquor, on licensed premises by some person other than the occupier, or a servant in such premises, shall be evidence that such liquor was sold to the person consuming or about to consume the same by or on behalf of the holder of such licence.

If any vendor of ginger or other beer, soda water, lemonade, or the like drinks, not being duly licensed, shall supply liquors to mix or be taken with such drink, he shall be deemed to have sold such liquor.

Any person failing to produce his licence or give other satisfactory proof of being licensed shall be deemed to be unlicensed.—What constitutes evidence of unlawful sale of liquor.

LXXXIV. In any proceeding against any person for selling, or allowing to be sold, any liquors without a licence, such person shall be deemed to be unlicensed unless he shall produce his licence or give other satisfactory proof of his being licensed. The fact of any person not holding a licence having any sign or notice importing that he is licensed upon or near his premises, or having a house or premises fitted up with a bar or other place containing bottles, casks, or vessels, so displayed as to induce a reasonable belief that liquor is sold or served therein, or of their being on such premises liquor concealed, or more liquor than is reasonably required for the persons residing therein, shall be deemed *prima facie* evidence of the unlawful sale of liquor by such person.

Manner in which offence shall be set forth in any summons or information.

XCIII. Any person may prosecute any offender for contravening the provisions of this Act: and in any summons or information it shall be sufficient to set forth the offence charged in the words of this Act or in similar words without inserting or negativing any exception, exemption, or qualification, but any such exception, exemption, or qualification may be proved by the defendant.

Any portion not exceeding one-half of any penalty imposed and
recovered may be awarded to prosecutor.

XCIV. The court before which any offence against this Act shall be
prosecuted may direct that any portion not exceeding one-half of any
penalty imposed and recovered, shall be paid or awarded to any person
who may have given such information as shall have led to the conviction
of the offender; and when any prosecution shall have been conducted by
any field-cornet one-half of the penalty imposed and recovered shall be
awarded to such field-cornet as remuneration for his trouble in conducting
such prosecution.

POWERS AND DUTIES OF OFFICERS OF JUSTICE.

Production of licence within a reasonable time after production is demanded.

LXIV. Every holder of a licence under this Act shall produce such
licence within a reasonable time after production therof is demanded by
any resident magistrate, justice of the peace, excise officer, chief constable,
or member of any police force.

Duties of Police with regard to licensed premises.

LXX. It shall be the duty of the chief constable or chief officer of the
police to report to the licensing court any licensed premises which are
out of repair, or have not reasonable accommodation, or proper or
sufficient sanitary or drainage requirements, and any case in which the
holder of a licence shall be of drunken habits, or shall keep a disorderly
house.

Right of entry on licensed premises.

LXXI. Any chief constable or officer of police, or any constable or
policeman authorized in writing by the resident magistrate, chief constable, or police officer, may, during the hours for which the premises are
licensed, enter on any such premises, and inspect and examine every
room and part of such premises, for the purpose of reporting, as in the
last preceding section is required, as to the state and condition of the
premises.

Any licensed person may be ordered to close his premises during a riot.

LXXXI. Where any riot or tumult occurs or is expected to occur in
any place, the resident magistrate, or any two justices of the peace, may
order any or every licensed person in or near such place to close his
premises during any time which such magistrate or justices may see fit.

Force may be used in carrying out such order.

LXXXII. Any person acting by order of any resident magistrate or
two justices of the peace may use such force as may be necessary for
closing such premises : Any person resisting or obstructing the execution
of any such order, and any licensed person selling liquor in contravention
of such order, shall upon conviction be liable to a penalty not exceeding
fifty pounds.

Any place or vehicle in which liquor is not authorized to be sold may
be searched under warrant issued by any Justice of the Peace.

LXXXVII. Any justice of the peace, if satisfied by information on
oath that there is reasonable ground to believe that liquor has been or is
being sold or kept for sale at any place, whether a building or not, in
which or where such liquor is not authorized to be sold, or in any vehicle,
may grant a warrant under his hand by virtue whereof it shall be lawful
for any constable or member of a police force at any hour within a time
to be stated in such warrant, or if no time be stated, within fourteen days
from the date thereof, to enter, and if need be by force, the place or vehicle
named in the warrant, and every part thereof, and search for liquor
therein, and to seize and remove any liquor found therein which there is
reasonable ground to believe or suppose is in such place or vehicle for the
purpose of unlawful sale, and the vessels containing such liquor.

WIDOW'S Pension Act, amended and altered. Act 14, 1882.
WIFE, crime against. Husband may prosecute. Ordinance 40,
1828, sect. 16. See also Act, 20, 1856, sect. 51, in case of S. Law, p. 356.
refusal.
WILD Ostriches Act, 12, 1870.
—— Ostriches Protection Act, 15, 1875. Removal of eggs by
servant of co-proprietor of farm not punishable. Buchanan,
1875, part 4, page 137.
WILFULLY harbouring idle or disorderly persons. Act 23,
1879, sect. 3.
WILLS. No legitimate portion can be claimed as a right out
of estate of any person dying. Act 23, 1874, sect. 2. Vol. 5, p. 57.
—— Person making will may disinherit or omit to mention
child, parent, relative, or descendant. *Ibid.* Sect. 3.
—— Stamps to be used for. Act 3, 1864. R. of C., page 313.
—— attesting of. See " Attesting."
WITNESS, if a savage, testimony may be accepted without
oath. Magistrate to enjoin him to speak the truth, the whole
truth, &c., &c. Penalty of perjury in this case, in event of
false statement. Ordinance 14, 1846, sect. 6. R. of C., page
427.
—— in *criminal* cases may be called on to find bail for
appearance, and committed to prison in default of bail.
Ordinance 73, 1830, sect. 20; Stat. Law, page 378. Ordinance
40, 1828, sect. 31. S. Law, p. 360.
—— in *criminal* cases. Deposition of, admitted at trial.
1st. If he shall have since died.
2nd. Or been kept away by prisoner.
3rd. Or, if he is too ill to travel, provided prisoner had
opportunity to cross-examine. Sect. 41, Ordinance 72, 1830 ;
Also Act 17, 1874. S. Law, p. 162.
4th. Dying declaration (made under apprehension of
death, admissible). Sect. 43, Ordinance 72, 1830.
—— in *criminal* cases. Expenses attending prosecutions
allowed except for common assault, verbal injuries, or tresspass.
Also prisoner's witnesses under certificate of poverty. R. of C.,
page 479.
—— in *criminal* cases. One credible witness sufficient except
in perjury. Ordinance 72, 1830, sect. 32 & 33.
—— in *criminal* cases. Summoned and not appearing.
Fine £5 or 14 days. Act 20, 1856, sched. B., rule 75, and
Ibid. sched. B., rule 18, for amount of fine.
—— in *civil* cases. Testimony of deceased or absent, taken
and admissible, if allowed by English Law. Ordinance 72,
1830, sect. 42.
—— in *civil* cases. Evidence of one credible witness sufficient. *Ibid.* Sect. 32 & 33.
—— in *civil* cases. Summoned and reasonable expenses paid.
Fine for not appearing, £5 or 14 days. Act 20, 1856, rule 18,
page 212.
—— material, non-appearance of, having been duly summoned.
R. M. may postpone without hearing witnesses, or may take

evidence of witnesses present and then postpone. Act 20, 1856, rule 19, page 212.

WITNESS must be sworn before giving evidence. Ordinance
S. Law, p. 410. 72, 1830, sect. 5.

but in case of youth, ignorance, &c. See Act 4, 1861, sect. 12.

may be questioned first by R. M. as to his knowledge of the obligation of an oath. Act 20, 1856, rule 21, page 213, R. of C.

expenses. See Ordinance 59, 1829, and 69, 1830.

———— expenses of material, to be allowed in absolution from instance. Buchanan, 1875, part 1, page 3.

———— if material, expense of, to be allowed whether called or not. *Ibid.* Page 6.

———— expenses of, allowed, when admission made did not necessitate calling witness. Buchanan, 1875, part 2, page 75.

———— expenses of, *disallowed* if evidence of witness inadmissible. Buchanan, 1875, part 2, page 77.

———— must be recalled when a new trial is had.

———— Insolvent is competent as. Statute Law, page 566, sect. 51.

———— Attesting wills, powers of attorney, &c. See "Attesting."

WRONG side in driving, injury caused by. Act 27, 1882, sect. 7, paragraphs 1 and 2.

WRONGFUL dismissal. Clerk or assistant to stationer, not a servant under Masters and Servants Act. Buchanan, 1879, part 1, page 22.

———— dismissal. Insufficient notice alone does not give action for.

misconduct of a servant is a defence to. Buchanan, 1879, part 4, page 217.

APPENDIX.

LAW OF CUSTOMS, 1884.

Alphabetically arranged.

BREAK Open Locks. Fast places—Officer above.

BRIBE offered, &c., to Officer of Customs. Penalty £200, p. 182, sect. 56.

CALLING Steamer without cargo need not report. Cir. 13/81, 5/7/81. Letter to be written.

CARRIAGES, Cattle Vessels, Boats made use of in running goods, forfeited, p. 181, sect. 54.

—— Number to be stated.

CARTRIDGES. Duty leviable on full value, and 6d. per lb. on gunpowder contained. Cir. 32/83.

CHARGE Books of Officers. Inspection of. Cir. 23/82, 9/11/83; 21/82, 8/11/82.

CIGARETTES chargeable as manufactured tobacco on total weight. Gross weight. Cir. 17/80.

CIGARS, Cigarettes, &c., to be weighed. Cir. 24/7; 8/83.

—— duty leviable on. Cir. 26/80, 18/12/80.

CLAIMING seized goods, p. 183, sect. 57. Notice in writing, or action cannot be brought against Officer for seizure.

CLEARANCE, and Transit coastwise, p. 242, sect. 6, to be handed in at Customs 24 hours after arrival, p. 242, sect. 8.

—— of Vessels to load at port where no Officer of Customs, p. 175, sect. 33.

COASTING Vessels may be boarded and searched, p. 243, Vol. 4, sect. x.

COASTWISE. Goods and passengers may be conveyed in foreign vessels, p. 240, Vol. 4, sect. 1.

—— Intercolonial trade to be, p. 241, Vol. 4.

—— Vessels arriving viâ Cape Ports to be treated as in Shipping Return, 9/4/83.

COLLUSIVE seizure, p. 182, sect. 56.

COLONIAL produce and duty paid goods may be shipped to vessel containing original cargo not coastwise, p. 241, Vol. 4, sect. 3.

CONDITIONS of Bond. Warehoused goods to be cleared in accordance with, p. 178, sect. 43.

CONFIDENTIAL Report on Officers every year. Cir. 15, 18/9/80.

CORDAGE. Cwt. to be stated.

CORDIAL. Lime juice, ad valorem. Cir. 15 Nov. 1878.

CORKS and Bungs. Number of gross.

CORN Grain, Meal and Pulse. lbs. to be stated.

—— Brandy. Spirits unsweetened. Cir. 21, 18/7/83.

COSTS in Action for Condemnation. Claimant to give security for, p. 185, sect. 67.

CROWN. Goods imported by, and subsequently sold, liable to duty, p. 167, xvi. See Circular 11/80, 31/7/80. Duty will not be leviable on stores sold by Crown Land Department.

DECLARATION of Officer of Customs, p. 164, Vol. 4, iv.

—— of Value of Imported Goods to be signed in presence of Officer may be on oath, p. 171, sect. 26.

DEFICIENCY in Bonded goods to be paid for, p. 177, sect. 40. (See Exceptions.)

—— on goods entered for Exportation, p. 180, sect. 47.

DEFINITION of terms employed in Customs' Act, No. 10 of 1872, p. 163, Vol. 4, sect. ii.

DESTROYED accidentally. Goods, duty remitted, p. 180, sect. 47.

DISMISSAL of Officer taking unauthorized fees, p. 164, Vol. 4, sect. v.

DROITS of Admiralty Cir. 3/82, 1/3/82.

DUTIES to be paid into Treasury, p. 167, Vol. 4, sect. xviii.

DYNAMITE, &c., 4d. per lb. Act 10, 1883.

EMPLOYMENT. Candidates for, Christian names in full. Cir. 9/81, 5/4/81.

ENQUIRY by principal Officer. Principal Officer may administer oath, p. 165, Vol. 4, sect. vi.

ENTRY outwards of vessels, p. 169, sect. xxi.

—— of goods before landing or shipping and warrants granted, p. 170, sect 23.

—— to be made within 14 days after arrival of vessel, p. 173, sect. 28.

EVIDENCE in suit for penalties, p. 184, sect. 63.

EXAMINATION of goods at Importer's expense, p. 166, Vol. 4, sect. xiii.
―――― on which deficiency not to be made good, p. 177, sect. 40.
EXAMINING Officer to check and compute all duties on entries presented to them. Cir. 18, 7/6/83.
EXPEDITE business. Officer is to use efforts to. Cir. 3, 19/2/81.
EXPORTATION Bond for double duty. Conditions of Bond, p. 179, sect. 44.
EXTRA attendance at Queen's and Bonded warehouses. Cir. 7, 10/12/79.
FALSIFICATION of documents, false oath or declaration, penalized, sect. 76, p. 188.
FEMALE to be searched only by female, p. 181, sect. 52.
FERNS from Natal, &c. Cir. 25/80, 16/12/82.
FERRYING Officers at Port Alfred £4 p. a.
FIRE. Goods destroyed by. *See* Destroyed in Bonded Warehouses. Cir. 28/81, 14/12/81.
FIREARMS. Notice concerning to be posted. Cir. 2, 11 Aug. 1883.
―――― and Ammunition. Treaty as to export. Cir. 16/80, 2/10/80.
FORFEITURES. Prohibited goods, sect. xiv. p. 166; goods imported or exported at place not proclaimed Free Warehousing Port, p. 166, Vol. 4, sect. xv.; goods sold after importation by Crown or person exempted, p. 167, sect. xvi.; goods landed not extract report, p. 169, sect. xx.; goods laden, or waterborne, or unladen, declared forfeited, p. 170, sect. 23; goods entered to be warehoused or taken out of.
FORMS of Entries, &c. Schedule, pp. 189, 190-206.
―――― Coastwise Schedule, p. 243, Vol. 4.
FREE Warehousing Ports. Governor may proclaim, p. 166, Vol. 4, sect. xv.
―――― Entry for short landing goods. Cir. 27/80.
FULL Report will not be sent. Cir. 8, 1/4/81.
GENERAL Bond by proprietor of warehouse, p. 176, sect. 38.
―――― issue to Suit. Officer of Customs may plead and give special matter in evidence, p. 185, sect. 69.
GINGER Ale. Extract, mixed spirits, Cir. 21, 18/7/83.
―――― Wine. Extract wine. Cir. 21, 18/7/83.
GLASS, Window. Cubic feet to be stated.
GLUCOSE is unrefined sugar. Cir. 11/82, 12/6/82.
GOLDEN Syrup, *ad valorem.* Cir. 29/80, 12/80.
GOVERNOR may declare free warehousing ports, *id. est.* ports into or from which goods may be imported or exported, p. 166, Vol. 4, sect. xv.
―――― to manage duties, p. 167, Vol. 4, sect. xvii.
―――― may restore seized goods to owner, p. 187, sect. 75.
GREEN Ginger Cordial (mixed spirit). Cir. 21, 18/7/83.
GUNPOWDER. Arms or munitions of war from any place not U. K. or British possessions may be prohibited, p. 166, Vol. 4, sect. xiv.
HATS. Number of dozen to be stated.
HINDERING, molesting, opposing, or obstructing Officer of Customs making seizure, forfeits £200, p. 182, sect. 55.
HOLIDAYS. Sunday, Christmas Day, Good Friday, New Year's Day, Fast or Thanksgiving Day, appointed, and H.M. Birthday, p. 165, Vol. 4, sect. ix.
HOPS. Cwt. to be stated.
HOURS of Attendance. Governor to appoint, p. 165, Vol. 4, sect. viii.
HOVERING vessel may be boarded, and brought into port, p. 180, sect. 50.
IMPROPER Seizure. On owner or claimant, not on seizing officer, p. 184, sect. 64.
INCREASE of Duties proposed, Act 1, 1864, Vol. 3.
INDECENT or obscure prints, photos, paintings, books, cards, &c., prohibited, p. 166, Vol. 4, sect. xiv.
INDEMNITY for refusal to deliver goods, Act 1, 1864, Vol. 3.
INSTRUCTIONS to Outdoor Officers. Cir. 21, 8/11/82.
―――― to Outdoor Officers, 8 April, 1880.
INVOICE may be required by officer, p. 172.
―――― Value of Cases. Cir. 6, 28/3/83.
IRON. Weight to be given.

JELLIES. Calves foot, lemon, orange, vanilla, charge as confectionery (12s. 6d.). Cir. 28, 4/9/83.

LANDED. Goods duty paid must be landed, or if sent on in vessel to be treated as not duty paid. Cir 5, 20/2/83.

LANDING or Shipping goods. Entry to be made before, p. 170, sect. 23.

LAST pay Certificate to be furnished by officer whose station is changed. Cir. 7, 27/2/83. 8/6/82. Col. Off.

LEAD. Weight to be given.

LEATHER Manufactures. Entries to state, not including boots and shoes. Cir. 16/83, 22/5/83.

LEAVE of Absence. Medical certificate over two days. Cir. 10/1883, 10/4/83.

LIMEJUICE Cordial. *Ad valorem,* letter, Nov. 78.

LIVE Stock. Importation of Madagascar and Inhambane, exempted from operation of Proc. 8/10/79. Cir. 4/80, 6/2/82.

LOCKS. Duty in case of fire. Bonded warehouse. Cir. 28 of 1881, 14/12/81.

MAIL Steamers clearing for extra Colonial ports to be considered coasters, p. 241, Vol. 4, sect. ii.

MALT. Number of quarts to be stated.

MANIFEST or B.L. to be deposited by vessel calling, p. 168, Vol. 4, sect. xix.

MARBLE. Stones, whether rough, dressed, or polished. Free if for building or ornamental purposes (includes tombstones). Cir. 14/81, 6/7/81.

METHYLIC Alcohol. Spirit duty. Cir. 5/82.

MOLASSES. 8s. per 100 lbs. Act. 26/80.

NAPHTHA. In its crude state, oil duty, Cir. 5/82; in purified state, "Methylic Alcohol," spirits unsweetened. Cir. 5/82.

NOTICE of Action to be given to Officer of Customs, p. 185, sect. 68.

NUTS (excepting cocoa-nuts). Lbs. to be stated.

OATH may be administered by Collector or P. O. in enquiry, p. 165, sects. v., vi.

——— as to value of goods may be required by Collector or other proper officer, p. 172, sect. 26.

OBSTRUCTING, molesting, hindering officer in making seizure, penalty £200, p. 182, sect. 55; under writ of assistance, p. 183, sect. 59.

OFFICER of Customs performing certain work to be considered proper officer, p. 163, Vol. 4, sect. iii.

——— guilty of collusion not to seize. Penalty £500, p. 182, or imprisonment for 5 years.

——— may be stationed on board ship, p. 166, Vol. 4, sect. x.; must be lodged and fed, penalty £20, sect. xi.

OFFICIAL Correspondence. Mode of conducting. Cir. 23/81, 25/11/81.

ONUS Probandi. Of seizure being improper, of payment of duties or lawful importation, &c., on owner or claimants of seized goods, p. 184, sect. 64.

ORANGE Bitters. Mixed spirits. Cir. 21, 18/7/83.

OVERTIME. Port Alfred regulated. Cir. 10, 22/12/80.

PARTICULARS of Report, p. 168, sect. 19.

——— of Bill of Entry, p. 170, sect. 24.

——— of Bill of Entry. Goods must correspond or will be forfeited, p. 174, sect. 31.

PASSENGERS' Luggage. Notice regarding to be posted. Cir. 11, 16/6/81.

PENALTIES, action for, barred after 3 years, p. 187, sect. 73.

PERMIT of R. M. before shipment of gunpowder, &c. Cir. 5, 23/3/81.

PIPES, iron and earthenware. Cwt. to be given.

· ——— Mounted, &c. Cir. 33, 5/10/83.

PITCH and Rosin. Cwt. to be given.

PLATE and Silver. Oz. to be given.

PLATED Ware, &c. 20%.

PLEA of Tender made by Officer, p. 186, sect. 71.

PORTS made free warehousing, p. 174, sect. 32.

——— Governor may establish, for limited purposes, p. 175, sect. 33.

POST Office Certificate. Cir. 13/82, 15/6/82.

STOP cases for examination. Cir. 19/80, 16/10/80.
STORES. List of unconsumed, p. 168, sect. xix. Victualliug bill, p. 169, sect. 21.
———— Value of to be shown.   Treated as exports.   Cir. 26/81, 10/12/81.
STORING of bonded goods, p. 175, sect. 35.
STOWAGE of Bonded goods as Collector may direct, p. 175, sect. 36.
STRAWBERRY Syrup. Mixed spirits. Cir. 21, 18/7/83.
SUIT against Officer of Customs barred, p. 182, sect. 57.
SULPHUR, Flowers of. Cwt. to be stated.
TAR. Number of gallons to be stated.
TEMPORARY Clerk or Officer. Payment of. Cir. 14/83, 17/5/83.
———— Queen's warehouse, p. 170, sect. 23 ; p. 174, sect. 30.
TENDER of amends by seizing Officer, p. 186, sect. 71.
TIN. Number of lbs. to be stated.
TRADE Marks. British marks or brands on articles of foreign manufacture prohibited to be imported, p. 166, Vol. 4, sect. xix.
TRANSHIPMENT of bonded goods, p. 179, sect. 44; without actual landing, p. 179, sect. 45; bond under 37 sect. dispensed with ; bond for estimated value, p. 179, sect. 46 ; record of list to be kept and return to be sent in. Cir. 4, 14 February, 1883.
———— of Goods. Cir. 19, 16/6/83.
TRANSHIPPED goods liable to wharfage. Cir. 11/83, 2/5/83.
UNAUTHORIZED Fees. Receipt by Officer, dismissal, p. 164, Vol. 4, sect. v.
UNCONSUMED Stores. List of to be deposited, p. 168.
UNDERVALUATION of Goods, p. 172, sect. 26.
———— undervalued, 60% forfeited, p. 173.
———— Refusal of importer to pay duties.
———— assessed by sect. 26, p. 173, sect. 27.
UNSOUND Wine. Admitted as vinegar.
VALUE of Goods. Declaration by importer, p. 171, sect. 26.
———— at port whence imported. Cir. 30, 10/9/83.
VERMOUTH is rated as wine. Cir. 21, 18/7/83.
VESSELS Inwards and Outwards. Weekly return to be sent in. Cir. 18/80, 9/10/80.
VINE Cuttings. Importation prohibited. Cir. 9/80, 6/80.
VINEGAR. Delivery of unsound wine as, p. 178.
V. O. C. for increase duties dispensed with. Cir. 31, 12/9/83.
WAREHOUSED Goods. Account to be taken of on landing. Book to be kept, p. 177, sect. 39.
———— Deficiency. Duty to be paid on, 177; 10% to be added to value. Cir. 3, 26/1/83.
WAREHOUSING Entries. Bond for double duty to be given, p. 175, sect. 37.
WEIGHING, &c., of goods at expense of importer, p. 166, vol. 4, sect. xiii.
WEIGHTS and Measures to be those by Law established in Colony, p. 167, sect. xvii.
WIDOWS' Pension Fund. Certificate. Cir. 6/81, 15/3/81.
WINE. Unsound admixture of vinegar or salt with and delivery as vinegar, p. 178, sect. 42.
WRECK to be reported by telegram, and full particulars by letter. Cir. 10, 11/4/83.
WRECKS, Wreckage, &c. Cir. 3/82, 1/3/82.
WRIT of Assistance, p. 183, sect. 58; obstructing Officer acting under, p. 183, sect. 59.

APPENDIX.87

FORMS USED IN CRIMINAL CASES.

FORMS.

SUMMONS.

1 Court of the Resident Magistrate for
       To   Messenger of the Court.
You are hereby required and directed, in Her Majesty's name, on the sight hereof, to summon   that he appear personally before this Court at   on the   Day of   at   o'clock in the forenoon, there to answer and abide the Judgment of this Court, upon the complaint and information of   Esquire, who prosecutes in the name and on behalf of Her Majesty, that the said   did on or about the   and such persons (if any) as you shall be required by the said   to summon on his behalf, that they, and each of them, be and appear personally, on the day and at the place aforesaid, to testify all they, and each of them, know concerning the said Charge.
    Serve on each of them, the said   a copy of this Summons, and return to the Court, on that Day, what you have done hereon.
    Given under my Hand, at   this   Day of   18
Clerk of the said Court.   Resident Magistrate of the said District.

---

2 Court of the Resident Magistrate for
       To   Messenger of the Court.
You are hereby required, in Her Majesty's name, to summon that they, and each of them, appear personally before this Court at   on the   day of   next, at   o'clock in the forenoon, to testify and declare all they, and each of them, know concerning a certain Charge preferred by the Public Prosecutor against   or
    Serve on each of them the said   a Copy of this Summons, and return to this Court, on that day, what you have done hereon.
    Given under my hand, at   this   day of   18
    Resident Magistrate of the said District.

INDICTMENT.
[A]
3   ORDINARY JURISDICTION.
No.   ·
18   .
In the Court of the Resident Magistrate for the District of
Holden at   before   , Esquire, Resident Magistrate for the said District, on the   day of   , 18 .   *versus*   Charged with the crime of   . In that upon (or about) the   day 18 , and at (or near)   in the said District, the said   did wrongfully and unlawfully
The Prisoner being arraigned, pleaded   Judgment,
Sentence,

[B]
4   REMITTED UNDER ORDINARY JURISDICTION.
No. .
18   .
In the Court of the Resident Magistrate for the District of
Holden at   before   , Esquire, Resident Magistrate for the said District, on the   day of   I   *versus*   charged with the crime of   In that upon (or about) the   day of   · 18 , and at (or near)   in the said District, the said   did wrongfully and unlawfully

The case having been remitted by the Attorney (or Solicitor) General,
to be tried by the Resident Magistrate under his ordinary jurisdiction, by
letter dated   , and received   , the Prisoner was this day
arraigned under Section 29 of Act No. 3 of 1861, and   pleaded
Judgment,   Sentence,

[C]

5   SUMMARY TRIAL UNDER ACT 17 OF 1867.
                              No. .
                               18 .
In the Court of the Resident Magistrate for the District of
   Holden at   before   , Esquire, Resident Magistrate for the said
District, on the   day of   18 .   *versus*   Charged
under the provisions of Act 17 of 1867, with the crime of Theft of Cattle.
In that upon (or about) the   day of   , 18 , and at (or near)
      in the said District, the said   did wrongfully and unlawfully
   The Prisoner, being arraigned, pleaded
   The following evidence was adduced, in the presence and hearing of the
Prisoner, then in   sound and sober senses ;   Judgment,
Sentence,

[D]

6   REMITTED UNDER ACT 17 OF 1867.—PLEA OF NOT GUILTY.
                              No. .
                               18 .
In the Court of the Resident Magistrate for the District of
   Holden at   before   , Esquire, Resident Magistrate for the said
District, on the   day of   18 .   *versus*   Charged,
under the provisions of Act 17 of 1867, with the crime of Theft of Cattle,
in that upon (or about) the   day of   , 18 , and at (or near)
      in the said District, the said   did wrongfully and unlawfully
   This case having been remitted by the Attorney (or Solicitor) General,
to be tried by the Resident Magistrate under the increased jurisdiction
conferred by Act 17 of 1867, by letter dated   , and received   ,
the Prisoner was this day arraigned, and pleaded   Judgment, .
Sentence,

[E]

7   REMITTED UNDER ACT 12 OF 1860, AND ACT 17 OF 1867.—
                         PLEA OF GUILTY.
                              No. .
                               18 .
In the Court of the Resident Magistrate for the District of
   Holden at   , before   , Esquire, Resident Magistrate of the
said District, on the   day of   , 18 .   *versus*
Charged with the crime of   In that upon (or about) the   day
of   , and at (or near)   in the said District, the said
did wrongfully and unlawfully
   This case having been remitted by the Attorney-General (or Solicitor)
under Act No. 12 of 1860 (or 17 of 1867), by letter dated   and
received   the Magistrate caused the Prisoner to be this day brought
before him, in the terms of Act No. 3 of 1861, Section 25, and informed
him that the preparatory examination on the charge of   in the course
of which he had voluntarily admitted his guilt, had been remitted back to
this Court. The Prisoner being asked whether he had anything to say
why sentence should not now be passed upon him for the offence of which
he had confessed himself guilty, stated   Judgment,   Sentence,

8   REMITTED UNDER ACT 12 OF 1860.—PLEA OF GUILTY.
No.   .
18   .
In the Court of the Resident Magistrate for the District of
Holden at   , before   , Esquire, Resident Magistrate of the
said District, on the   day of   18   .   *versus*   Charged
with the crime of   In that upon (or about) the   day of   ,
and at (or near)   in the said District   the said   did wrongfully and unlawfully
      This case having been remitted by the Attorney-General (or Solicitor)
under Act No. 12 of 1860, by letter dated   and received   the
Magistrate caused the Prisoner to be this day brought before him, in the
terms of Act No. 3 of 1861, Section 25, and informed him that the
preparatory examination on the charge of   in the course of which he
had voluntarily admitted his guilt, had been remitted back to this Court.
The Prisoner being asked whether he had anything to say why sentence
should not now be passed upon him for the offence of which he had confessed himself guilty, stated   Judgment,   Sentence,

9   WARRANT OF COMMITTAL TO GAOL.
Court of the
To the Gaoler of Her Majesty's Gaol at
      Whereas the undermentioned Prisoners were this day respectively and
duly convicted before me of the several offences undermentioned, and were
for the said offences sentenced by me to undergo the several Punishments
respectively affixed to their Names: This is, therefore, to require you, in
Her Majesty's Name, to receive the said several Prisoners into your
Custody, and there safely keep them until they shall have undergone the
said Punishment, or shall be otherwise lawfully discharged therefrom.

Prisoner's Name.	Sentence.	Of what Offence Convicted.
	.	

Given under my hand at   this   day of   18   .
Witness,   Clerk of the said Court.

10   WARRANT OF COMMITMENT FOR FURTHER EXAMINATION.
District of   To the Gaoler of the   Gaol.
      These are to command you to receive into your Gaol the Body of
who is hereby recommitted for further examination,   and to keep the
said   in your custody until brought before me, on the   day of
      for the purpose aforesaid.
      Given under my hand at   this   day of   18   .

11   WARRANT OF COMMITMENT FOR TRIAL.
District of   To the Gaoler of the   Gaol.
      These are to command you to receive into your Gaol the Body of
charged on the Oath of   and others, before me, with the crime of
      and to keep the said   in your custody in the said Gaol, till
brought to Trial for the said Crime, or liberated in due course of Law.
      Given under my hand at   this   day of   18   .

12   WARRANT OF LIBERATION.
District of   To the Gaoler of the   Gaol.
These are to command you to liberate from your custody the Body of
         committed thereto by Warrant dated   unless lawfully detained
otherwise than by the said Warrant.
Given under my hand at   this   day of   18   .

13   WARRANT TO LEVY FINE.
Court of the
                    To   Messenger of the Court.
Whereas   was on the   day of   18   duly convicted
before me   Esq., Resident Magistrate for   of having
and was sentenced by me to pay for this said Offence, the Sum of
This is therefore to require you (or one of you), that of the Goods and
Chattels of the said   in this   you cause to be levied and raised
the Penalty aforesaid, together with your Charges about the same; and
have that Money before me on the   day of   next, to be rendered
to the Clerk of this Court,—and return on that day this Warrant, with
what you shall have done hereon.
For which this shall be your Warrant.
Given under my hand at Cape Town, this   day of   18   .
                              Clerk of the Court.

14   WARRANT TO ARREST AND IMPRISON IN DEFAULT OF PAYMENT.
Cape of Good Hope.
          Esquire, Resident Magistrate for   To
Whereas   was on the   day of   18   , duly convicted before
me of   and was adjudged to pay a Fine of   Pounds Sterling:
And whereas it appears by   that the said   hath not sufficient
Goods to satisfy the said Conviction;—These are therefore to command
you, that you apprehend the said   and deliver him over into the
Custody of the Keeper of Her Majesty's Gaol at
Given under my hand at   this   day of   18   .

15   WARRANT OF COMMITMENT TO PRISON IN DEFAULT OF PAYMENT.
Resident Magistrate for
          To the Keeper of Her Majesty's Gaol at
Whereas   was on the   day of   18   , duly convicted before
me, of   and was adjudged to pay a Fine of   Pounds Sterling :
And whereas it appears by   that the said   hath not sufficient
goods to satisfy the said Conviction;—These are therefore to command
you, that you receive into your said Gaol the body of the said
and that you safely keep him in your custody in your said Gaol for the
term of   Days, unless the said Fine shall be sooner paid.
Given under my hand, at   , this   day of   18   .

16   WARRANT OF APPREHENSION.
          Esquire,   for the
To the Field-cornets, Constables, Police Officers, and other Officers of
the Law proper to the execution of Criminal Warrants.
Whereas, from information taken upon oath before me, there are
reasonable grounds for suspicion against   of   , that   did on
the   day of   commit the crime of
These are, therefore, in Her Majesty's Name, to command you that
immediately upon sight hereof you apprehend and bring the said   or
cause   to be apprehended and brought before   to be examined,
and to answer to the said information, and to be further dealt with
according to Law.
Given under my hand at   this   day of   18   .

17   SEARCH WARRANT.
Court of the
To
    Whereas it appears to me, by the information on Oath of   of
that the following Goods, to wit: have, within   days last past,
by some Person or Persons unknown, been feloniously taken, stolen and
carried away, out of the House of the said   at   aforesaid, and
that the said   hath probable cause to suspect, and doth suspect, that
the said Goods, or part thereof, are concealed in the Dwelling House of
    of   These are, therefore, in the name of our Lady the Queen,
to authorize and require you, with necessary and proper Assistants, to
enter, in the day time, into the said Dwelling House of the said   at
    aforesaid, and there diligently to search for the said Goods, and if
the same, or any part thereof, shall be found upon such Search, that you
bring the Goods so found, and also the Body of the said   . before me,
to be disposed of and dealt with according to Law.
    Given under my hand at   on the   day of   18 .

------

18   WARRANT OF REMOVAL.
To the Gaoler of   and   The Gaoler of
    Whereas application hath been made to me by the Clerk of the Peace
for this District, praying that   now a Prisoner in the Gaol of
charged with the crime of   be removed for   to the Gaol of
    These are therefore to command you, the Gaoler of   that you
cause the said   to be removed as aforesaid, and delivered to the
Gaoler of   who is hereby authorized and required to receive into his
Custody, the Body of the said   and him safely to detain until brought
before   for the District of   or liberated in due course of Law.
    Given under my hand at   this   day of   18 . .

------

19 WARRANT OF COMMITMENT FOR WANT OF SURETIES TO KEEP THE PEACE.
To   and also to the Keeper of Her Majesty's Gaol at   and others
whom it may concern.
    Whereas   came personally before me,   Esquire,   for the
. District of   aforesaid, on   day of .   and on his oath, informed
me that   did on the   day of   18 , and at   in the
District of   aforesaid,   and that from the above premises, he,
the Complainant, is afraid that the said   will do   some bodily
injury, And therefore prays that the said   may be required to find
sufficient Sureties to keep the Peace and be of good behaviour towards
him, this Complainant : And whereas the said Complainant also made oath
that   doth not make this complaint from any hatred, malice, or ill-
will, but merely for the preservation of   Person from injury : And
whereas the said   was this day brought and appeared before me to
answer the said complaint, and I have ordered and adjudged, and do
hereby order and adjudge, that the said   shall enter into   own
recognizance in the sum of   pounds sterling, with two sufficient
sureties in the sum of   each, to keep the Peace and be of good
behaviour towards Her Majesty and all her liege people, and especially
towards the said   for the space of   Calendar Months, now next
ensuing : And insomuch as the said   hath refused, and still refuses, to
enter into such Recognizance, and to find such Sureties as aforesaid :—I do
hereby require and command you, the said   forthwith to convey the
said   to the Gaol at   , and to deliver him to the Keeper thereof,
together with this Warrant. And I do also require and command you,

the said Keeper, to receive the said   ·   into your Custody in the said
Gaol, and   there safely to keep for the space of   Calendar
Months, unless he in the meantime enter into such Recognizance, with
such Sureties as aforesaid, to keep the Peace and be of good behaviour in
the manner and for the term above mentioned. Herein fail not.
    Given under my hand and seal at   this   day of   , 18 .

---

20   FORM OF GENERAL WARRANT TO BE ISSUED UNDER SECTION VI.
OF ACT 23 OF 1879.

To
    Whereas it has been made to appear to my satisfaction by information,
in writing upon oath that (*a*)   disorderly person named   are
upon the (*b*)   of   of   This is, therefore, to require you in
Her Majesty's Name to enter upon the said (*b*)   and in case
you shall there find the said   or any, or either of them, that you do
forthwith apprehend him (or them) and convey him (or them) before (*c*)
    at   to be dealt with according to Law.
    Given under my hand at   this   day of   , 18 .

                (*d*) _____

                (*e*) _____

  (*a*) Here insert "a" or "certain," as the case may be.
  (*b*) ,, ,, "Land" or "Premises."
  (*c*) ,, ,, "The Special Justice of the Peace at   ," or "Resident Magistrate of
  ," if Warrant signed by an ordinary Justice of the Peace, or "me" if signed by a
Resident Magistrate, or Special Justice of the Peace.
  (*d*) Signature of Officer by whom Warrant is issued.
  (*e*) "Resident Magistrate," "Justice of the Peace," or "Special Justices of the Peace," as the
case may be.

---

21   RECOGNIZANCE UNDER SECTION 55 OF ORDINANCE NO. 40.

    Be it Remembered, that on the   day of   18 , personally
came before me   and acknowledged themselves to owe to our Lady
the Queen, the said   the Sum of   and the said   the Sum
of   Sterling, of good and lawful Money of this Colony, to be made of
their several Goods and Chattels, Lands and Tenements, respectively, to
the use of our said Lady the Queen her Heirs and Successors, if the said
    shall make default in the Condition underwritten.
    The Condition of this Recognizance is, that if the said   shall appear
and answer to any Indictment that shall be presented against him in any
competent Court for the Crime   at any time within the space of Six
Months from the date hereof, and accept Service of the Indictment and
the Summons thereon, at   then this recognizance shall be null and
void, or else remain in full force.
    Taken and acknowledged the Day and Year above written before me,
the aforesaid   _____

---

22   RECOGNIZANCE TO KEEP THE PEACE.

    On the   Day of   in the Year of Our Lord One Thousand Eight
Hundred and Sixty-
    Appeared before me,   and acknowledged themselves to owe to our
Lady the Queen, to wit: the said   the Sum of   and the said
    the Sum of   and the said   the Sum of   of good and
lawful Money of this Colony, to be respectively made and levied of their
several Goods and Chattels, Lands and Tenements, to the use of our said
Lady the Queen, her Heirs and Successors, if he, the said   shall fail
in performing the Condition underwritten.
    The Condition of this Recognizance is, that if the said   shall keep

the Peace, and be of good behaviour towards the Queen and all her People, and especially towards then this Recognizance shall be null and void, or else to remain in full force.

Taken and acknowledged the Day and Year above written, before me, the aforesaid

_____

23 RECOGNIZANCE TO APPEAR BEFORE SUPREME COURT AND GRAND JURY.

Be it remembered, that on the Day of 18 , personally came before me Esquire, Resident Magistrate for the District of and acknowledged themselves to owe to our Lady the Queen, the said the Sum of Pounds Sterling, and the said and each in the sum of Pounds Sterling, of good and lawful Money of this Colony, to be made of their several Goods and Chattels, Lands and Tenements respectively, to the use of our said Lady the Queen, her Heirs and Successors, if the said shall make default in the Condition underwritten.

The Condition of this Recognizance is such, that if the said shall personally appear in the Supreme Court of this Colony, at any time within the space of Six Months, and then and there give such Evidence as he knoweth upon a Bill of Indictment, to be exhibited by Her Majesty's Attorney-General, who prosecutes for and on behalf of our Lady the Queen, to the grand jury, against for and in case the said Bill be found a true Bill, then if the said shall then and there give Evidence to the Jurors that shall pass on the Trial of the said upon the said Bill of Indictment, and not depart thence without leave of the Court,—and if the said shall accept Service of the Summons at then this Recognizance shall be null and void, or else remain in full force.

Taken and acknowledged the Day and Year above written, before me, the aforesaid

_____

24 WARRANT
Under in the 12th Section of Ordinance No. 9, 1846.

To
Whereas or other the owner or owners of a certain now this day been convicted before me of the offence of contravening the Ordinance No. 9, 1846; and I have thereupon adjudged that for the said offence do forfeit the sum of , this is, therefore, to authorise and require you to sieze and take possession of now belonging to the said , and to treat and dispose of the same as by the said Ordinance is provided, in order that of the same may be levied and made the said sum of together with your reasonable charges about the same; and for so doing this shall be your warrant. And return to me this warrant, endorsing thereupon what you shall have done under it.

Given under my hand at this day of 18 .

Road Magistrate.

_____

25 RECOGNIZANCE
Under the 22nd Section of Ordinance No. 9, 1846.

Before me on this day of 18 came and appeared who acknowledged himself to owe to our Lady the Queen the sum of , to be levied and made of his goods and chattels if he shall make default in the condition following :—

Whereas the said hath this day brought or caused to be brought before me, , a certain whereof is named as owner, com-

plaining that by, or by means of, the same, and at or near   the
Ordinance No. 9 of 1846, was   contravened; now the condition of
this recognizance is such that if the said   shall personally appear
before   between the hours of   and   o'clock in the forenoon
of the   day of   next ensuing, then and there to give evidence
touching and concerning the said alleged contravention, and shall not
depart without the leave of   , then this recognizance to be void.
Acknowledged before me as aforesaid.

26   PRELIMINARY EXAMINATION.

In the Case of the Queen *versus*   charged with   District
of
At   in the District of   on the   day of   18 , in
the presence of   for the said District, appeared   years of age,
born at   by trade or occupation   residing   who having
heard the evidence adduced in support of the charge made against
of having on the   day of   18 and at   in the District
of   and being asked what he will say in answer thereto, and being at
the same time cautioned that   is not obliged to make any statement
that may criminate, and that what   shall say may be used in
evidence against   declares
The above declaration was freely and voluntarily made by the
said   who was then in sound and sober senses, and having been read
over and interpreted to   adhered to the same, and affixed
thereto in the presence of the subscribing Witnesses and
Witnesses:

Prisoner's Name and Description.	Crime.	Date of Apprehension, if apprehended—if not, state that not in custody.	Whether committed for Trial or for further Examination, Committing Magistrate's Name, Date of Committal, and Prison to which committed.	Whether Bail found or not.	Remarks and Instructions of the Attorney-General.

27   SCHEDULE TO PRELIMINARY EXAMINATION.

List of Documents Transmitted with the Preparation Examinations.
Date of transmission of Documents.   Clerk of the Peace for

28   SUMMONS FOR WITNESS [INQUEST].

Inquest for the District of
          ·   To   Chief Constable.
You are hereby required, in Her Majesty's Name, to summon
of   that he appear before me on this the   day of   18 , in
the   noon, then and there to be examined at an Inquest touching
the death of
Herein fail not at your peril.
Dated at   this   day of   18 .

                                        Resident Magistrate.

29 WARRANT TO ARREST WITNESS FAILING TO ATTEND INQUEST.

To   Chief Constable, and other constables and officers of the law, proper to the execution of criminal warrants.

Whereas   of   who was duly summoned to appear before me at at   then and there to be examined at an Inquest touching the death of   and hath refused and neglected so to do, to the great delay and hindrance of justice; these are, therefore, in Her Majesty's Name, to command you, or some of you, to apprehend and bring before me the body of the said   that he shall be dealt with according to law; and for so doing this shall be your warrant.

Dated at   this   day of   18 .

_____ Resident Magistrate.

30 BILL OF EXPENSES.

Bill of Expenses.   Payable by the Crown.

PRELIMINARY EXAMINATION.

In the Case of   charged with the Offence of   .

Names of Witnesses.	Distance in Miles of Residence from Circuit or Magistrate's Court.	Number of Days allowed.	Rate per diem.		Amount.			We, the undersigned, do acknowledge to have received from the Civil Commissioner of the sums opposite to our respective Names, being the amount of Expenses allowed us in the above case.
			s.	d.	£	s.	d.	
		Total .						

Certificate of the Clerk of the Peace.

I hereby certify that the Witnesses named above were *necessarily* brought forward on the Preliminary Examination of this Case holden at   on the   day of   18   ; that the distances above stated are, to the best of my knowledge, correct, and that the number of Days allowed for the Travelling and attendance of each Witness is correct.   ·

(*Signature.*)

Certificate of the presiding Magistrate or Justice.

I hereby certify and allow the above, as the lawful and reasonable Expenses of the aforesaid Witnesses, amounting to   .

(*Signature.*)

Note.—In cases where the Clerk of the Peace has not attended, both the Certificates are to be signed by the Presiding Magistrate or Justice, being first duly filled up.

To be prepared, certified, and transmitted in *duplicate* and the sum to be inserted in the Certificate in writing.

H

31

BILL OF EXPENSES.

Bill of Expenses. Payable by the Crown.

DEFENCE.

In the Case of the Attorney-General *versus* .

Names of Witnesses.	Distance in Miles of Residence from Circuit or Magistrate's Court.	Number of Days allowed.	Rate per diem.		Amount.			We, the undersigned, do acknowledge to have received from the Civil Commissioner of the sums opposite to our respective Names, being the amount of Expenses allowed us in the above case.
			s.	d.	£	s.	d.	
		Total .						

Certificate of the Clerk of the Peace.

I hereby certify that the Witnesses named above were duly summoned, and appeared for the *Defence* on the trial of this Case, before the Court, holden at on the day of 18 , that the Distances above stated are, to the best of my knowledge, correct, and that the number of Days allowed for the Travelling and attendance of each Witness is correct.

(Signature.)

Certificate of the Magistrate or Registrar, by Order of the Court.

I hereby certify that the above Witnesses are entitled to receive payment of their expenses, and that the Rates allowed are reasonable—and the sum amounting to .

(Signature.)

To be prepared, certified, and transmitted in *duplicate*, and the sum to be inserted in the Certificate in writing. .

32

BILL OF EXPENSES.

Bill of Expenses. Payable by the Crown.

PROSECUTION.

In the Case of the Attorney-General *versus* .

Names of Witnesses.	Distance in Miles of Residence from Circuit or Magistrate's Court.	Number of Days allowed.	Rate per diem.		Amount.			We, the undersigned, do acknowledge to have received from the Civil Commissioner of the sums opposite to our respective Names, being the amount of Expenses allowed us in the above case.
			s.	d.	£	s.	d.	
		Total .						

Certificate of the Clerk of the Peace.

I hereby certify that the Witnesses named above were duly summoned and appeared for the *Prosecution* on the Trial of this Case, before the Court holden at   on the   day of   18 , that the distances above stated are, to the best of my knowledge, correct, and that the number of Days allowed for the Travelling and Attendance of each Witness is correct.

(*Signature.*)

Certificate of the Presiding Magistrate or Justice.

I hereby certify that the above Witnesses are entitled to receive payment of their Expenses, and that the rates allowed are reasonable—and the sum amounting to   .

(*Signature.*)

To be prepared, certified, and transmitted in *duplicate*, and the sum to be inserted in the Certificate in writing.

FIRE INQUEST SUMMONS FOR WITNESS.

" FIRE INQUESTS ACT, 1883."

Fire Inquest for the District of   .

To[1]   . You are hereby required in Her Majesty's Name to summon[2]   that he appear before me at   on the   day of   18 , at the hour of   in the fore[3]/after } noon, then and there to be examined at an inquest concerning a fire which occurred at on[4]   . Therein fail not at your peril.

Dated at   this   day of   18 .

Resident Magistrate or Justice of the Peace.

(1.) Name of the constable or person to whom the process is directed.
(2.) Describe him particularly.
(3.) As the case may be.
(4.) State the place and time.

FIRE INQUEST WARRANT TO ARREST WITNESS FAILING TO ATTEND.

" FIRE INQUESTS ACT, 1883."

Fire Inquest for the District of   .

To[1]   and constables and other officers of the law proper to the execution of criminal warrants.

Whereas[2]   of[3]   who was duly summoned to appear before me at[4]   then and there to be examined at an inquest concerning a fire which occurred at   on[5]   hath refused or neglected so to do, to the great delay and hindrance of justice, these are therefore in Her Majesty's Name to command you to apprehend and bring before me the body of the said   that he be dealt with according to Law : and for so doing this shall be your warrant.

Dated at   this   day of   18 .

Resident Magistrate or Justice of the Peace.

(1.) Name of person to whom the process is directed.
(2.) Insert name of person summoned.
(3.) Describe him particularly, as in the summons.
(4.) Name the place, as in the summons.
(5.) Stating the place and time.

FORMS USED IN CIVIL CASES.

FORMS.

1   POWER OF ATTORNEY TO SUE.

In the Court of the Resident Magistrate for the Division of hereby ordain, nominate and appoint with power of substitution, to be my lawful Attorney and Agent, and for me and in my name to take proceedings of Claim and Demand against and to institute proceedings for Civil Imprisonment, and to sign security bond as set forth in Rule 34, Act 20, 1856, to proceed to the final end and determination thereof, and generally for effecting the purposes aforesaid, to do, or cause to be done, whatsoever shall be requisite, as fully and effectually as might or could do if personally present and acting herein, hereby promising and agreeing to ratify, allow, and confirm all and whatsoever said Attorney and Agent shall lawfully do, or cause to be done, by virtue of these presents.

Given under hand, at this day of 18 , in the presence of the undersigned Witnesses.

As Witnesses :

       _____

2   SPECIAL POWER OF ATTORNEY.

Know all men whom it may concern, the Undersigned do hereby nominate, constitute, and appoint Attorney-at-Law, with power of substitution, to be true and lawful Attorney and Agent, in name, place, and stead, to and further, for effecting the purposes aforesaid, to do whatsoever shall be requisite, as fully, amply, and effectually, to all intents and purposes whatsoever, as might, or could, if personally present : hereby ratifying, allowing, and confirming, and promising and agreeing to ratify, allow, and confirm, all and whatsoever said Attorney and Agent shall, in name, lawfully do, or cause to be done, by virtue of these presents.

Given under hand, at this day of 18 , in the presence of the undersigned Witnesses. -

As Witnesses:

       _____

3   SUMMONS ON PROMISSORY NOTE.

Court of the Resident Magistrate for the District of
Messenger of the Court.

Summon in the District of (hereinafter styled the Defendant) that he appear before the Court of the Resident Magistrate of this District to be holden at , on the day of 18 , at 10 o'clock in the Forenoon, with Witnesses (if he have any) to show cause why he hath not paid to (hereinafter styled the Plaintiff) the Sum of which the said Plaintiff complains that he owes him being the amount of a certain Promissory Note bearing date the day of , 18 , and payable made and signed by the said Defendant, to and in favour of or order, and by together with the Interest thereon from the day of 18 , of which said Promissory Note the said Plaintiff is now the legal holder, and which not having been paid when due, was duly presented and dishonoured—which said Sum the said Defendant neglects or refuses to pay, wherefore the said Plaintiff prays that he may be adjudged to pay the same with Costs of suit.

And serve on the said Defendant a Copy of this Summons and of the said Promissory Note, and of the notice to produce on the other side hereof written, and return you on that day, to the said Court, what you have done on this Summons.

Plaintiff's Attorney.   Clerk of the said Court.

3a   INDORSEMENT OF NO. 3.
In the Court of the Resident Magistrate for the District of
In the suit between   Plaintiff, and   Defendant.
Take Notice that you are required to bring with you and produce at
the trial of this cause, certain the Letter of Demand, written and
addressed by me to you, bearing date the   day of
     To   Plaintiff's Attorney.
The above-named Defendant.

---

4   PLAINTIFF'S DECLARATION OR SUMMONS.
Court of the Resident Magistrate for
     •   Messenger of the Court.
     Summon   of   that he appear before the Court of the Resident
Magistrate of this District, to be holden at   on   the   day
of   18   at   o'clock in the Forenoon, with   Witnesses (if
he have any), to show why he hath not paid to   of   the Sum
of £   with Interest from   which the said   complains that
he owes   for   .
     And serve on the said   a Copy of this Summons   and return
you on that day, to the said Court, what you have done on this Summons.
         Clerk of the Court.

---

5   SUMMONS OR SUBPŒNA FOR WITNESS.
Court of the Resident Magistrate for
     Messenger of the Court.
     Summon   that, laying aside all and singular businesses and excuses,
they and each of them appear in person before this Court, at   on
the   day of   at   o'clock in the Forenoon, to testify and
declare all and singular those things which they, or any of them, know in
a certain case now depending in the said Court, between   Plaintiff,
and   Defendant, and that they, or either of them, by no means omit
so to do, at their peril.
     Serve on each of them the said   a Copy of this Summons, and
return to the said Court what you have done thereupon.
         Clerk of the said Court.

---

6   WARRANT TO ARREST WITNESS.
In the
To
Whereas   was duly summoned to appear before this Court on
the   day of   18   , to give evidence touching the Complaint
made by the   against   and has made default therein :—You are
hereby required to arrest the said   and to lodge him in the Gaol
at   , there to be detained until he shall be brought before this Court,
and there submit to be sworn, and to give Evidence touching the said
Complaint, or be discharged in due course of Law.
     Given under my hand, at   , this   day of

---

7   NOTICE TO DEFENDANT OF PROVISIONAL OR INTERLOCUTORY JUDGMENT.
Court of the Resident Magistrate for
     of   *against*   of
     Take Notice, that Interlocutory Judgment was this day given and
recorded against you in this Court, on behalf of the above-named Plaintiff,
for the Sum of   with interest thereon since the   together with
the Costs of Suit, for a certain Debt found to be owing by you to the
said   for
     And unless, on the   day of   next, at   o'clock in the
Forenoon, you show to the said Court sufficient cause to the contrary, the
said Judgment will become final and absolute, and Execution will be
issued thereon against you.   Clerk of the said Court.

8
BILL OF COSTS.

In the Court of the Resident Magistrate, Division of
Fees and Disbursements due to   Agent, in the Matter of
Plaintiff,   De¹endant.

Recording Plaint ..	..	..	..			
Issuing Summons ..	..	..	..			
Copies to serve	..	..	..			
Copy of Bill	..	..	..			
Copies of Documents filed	..	..				
Recording Appearance of Defendant	..					
Warrant of Execution	..	:	..			
Taking and Filing Security for Restitution						
Filing Agent's Authority	..					
Witnesses Examined	..	..				
Entering Judgment	..	..	..			
Do. Answer to Defendant	..	..				
Sheets of Evidence	..	..	..			
Orders of Court	..	..	..			
Notice of Judgment	..	..	..			
Taxation of Costs ..	..	..	..			
Paid for Stamps	..	..	..			
Writ and Stamp ..	..	..	..			
Messenger Fees	..	..	..			
Witness Expenses..	..	..				
Agent's Fees	..	..	..			
Attendance in Court..	..	..				
Demand	..	..	..			
Judgment ..	..	..	..			
Interest	..	..	..			

9
WRIT OF EXECUTION.

Court of the Resident Magistrate, District of
          Messenger of the Court.
Whereas, in a certain case in this Court, before me, wherein
of   was the Plaintiff, and   of   was the Defendant, the
said   on the   day of   last, by the Judgment of the Court,
recovered against the said   the sum of   together with the sum
of   for his Costs (which said Judgment had been duly affirmed on
Appeal,—if the case so be,—with the further sum of £   for Costs
thereon), as appears in the proceedings of the said Court :
This is, therefore, to require you, that of the movable Property of the
said   in this District, you cause to be levied and raised the Debt (or
Damages) and Costs aforesaid, together with your charges about the same,
and pay to the said Plaintiff the Debt (or Damages) and Costs aforesaid,
and return to the Clerk of this Court on or before the   day of
next, what you have done by virtue hereof, for which this shall be your
Warrant.
     Given under my hand at   this   day of   18 .
     Clerk of the Court.   Resident Magistrate.
[Sch. B., Sec. 40, Act No. 20, 1856.

10   NOTICE TO DEFENDANT OF ATTACHMENT OF PROPERTY.
Take Notice that I have this day seized and laid under Judicial Attachment the Articles comprised in the above Inventory, in pursuance of a
Warrant to me directed under the hand of   , Esq., Resident Magis-
trate for the District of   whereby I am required to cause to be levied
and raised of your Movable Property in this District the Sum of
and   Costs, recovered against you by the Judgment of the said
Court, in a certain case wherein   was the Plaintiff and yourself the
Defendant; and also for my Charges in and about the said Warrant.
                              Messenger of the said Court.
[Sec. 43, Sch. B, Act, 20, 1856.]

_____

11   BOND—SECURITY FOR GOODS ATTACHED.
                                                18 .
     of   Plaintiff   against   of   Defendant.
Whereas the said   on the   day of   last, by judgment
of the Court of the Resident Magistrate of the District of   ,
recovered against the said   the sum of   together with the sum
of   for Costs, in respect of a certain case in the said Court : And
whereas, by virtue of a certain warrant under the hand of   Esq.,
Resident Magistrate of the said District, bearing date on   directed
to   Messenger of the said Court, the said   has seized and laid
under attachment, in respect of the said judgment, and in respect to the
execution whereof the undermentioned articles, namely :

     Now, therefore, the said   and   of   a   as surety for
him, the said   severally undertake and promise to the said   that
the said goods shall not be made away with or disposed of, but the same
shall remain in possession of the said   under effect of the said
attachment, and shall be produced to the Messenger of the said Court, on
the   day of   next (the day appointed for sale), or any other
day when the same may be required, in order to be sold in execution of
the said judgment and expenses, if the same shall not be sooner satisfied
to the said   otherwise the said   hereby undertakes and binds
himself to pay and satisfy the said judgment, costs, and expenses, for and
on behalf of the said   .
     In witness whereof, the said   and   have hereunto set their
hands on this   day of   18 . .
     Messenger of the Court.
[Act 20, 1856. Sec. 44.]

_____

12   BOND—SECURITY DE RESTITUENDO.
                                                18 .
     of   , Plaintiff,   against   of   , Defendant.
Whereas the said   on the   day of   , recovered by
Judgment of the Court of the Resident Magistrate of the District
of   against the said   the sum of   together with the
sum of   for Costs, in a certain case before the said Court ; and
whereas the said Court has directed the said Judgment, notwithstanding
the said   has noted an Appeal against the same, to be carried into
execution, upon security being given for restitution ;
     Now, therefore, the said   and   of   , as surety for him,
the said   hereby severally undertake and bind themselves, jointly
and severally to refund and make due restitution of the above several
sums of   and   should the Judgment of the said Court be
reversed ; and further severally to conform to and execute such Judgment,
Order, or Decree as shall be given and pronounced upon or in respect of
such Appeal.

In witness whereof, the said   **and**   have hereunto set their hands, on this   day of   188 .
Clerk of the Court.
[Sch. B., Sec. 34, Act No. 20, 1856.]

---

13   BOND—INDEMNITY TO MESSENGER.

Whereas   Messenger to the Resident Magistrate for   , by virtue of Warrant of Execution to him directed, against the Goods and Chattels of   Issued out of the Court of the Resident Magistrate, at the suit of   , the said Messenger hath consented to seize and take into Execution certain Property or Goods, and to sell the same and pay over the money arising from the sale thereof, in satisfaction of the Debt and Costs, to the said Plaintiff, upon being sufficiently indemnified for so doing:
Now the Condition of this Obligation is such, that the said   , his Heirs, Executors, or Administrators, do and shall, and at all times hereafter will and sufficiently save himself and keep indemnified the said Messenger, of, from, and against all Losses, Costs, Charges, Damages, and Expenses which the said Messenger may sustain, suffer, bear, pay, expend, or be put into, for or by reason of, or means of seizing or selling the said Goods so seized and taken into Execution as aforesaid, or paying unto the said   the money arising from the sale thereof in satisfaction of the Debt and Costs so directed to be levied by the said Writ of Execution, and also of, from, and against all Actions, Suit or Suits, either in Law or Equity, which now are or may at any time hereafter be brought, commenced, or prosecuted by the said   or any other person whomsoever, against the said Messenger.

18 .

---

14   SUMMONS TO SHOW CAUSE AGAINST DECREE OF CIVIL IMPRISONMENT.

Court of the Resident Magistrate, District of   .
    To   , Messenger of the Court.
    Summon   of   that he appear before the Court of the Resident Magistrate of this District, to be holden at   on the   day of   next, at   o'clock in the Forenoon, to show why a Decree of Civil Imprisonment should not be made against him, at the suit of of   in respect of the non-payment of the sum of £   recovered against the said   by the said   by a Judgment of the said Court, bearing date the   day of   , 18 , and for the recovery of which sum a Warrant of Execution was, on the   day of   last past, duly sued out against the Movable Property of the said   and in regard to which Warrant a return has been duly made that no Movable Property has been found, whereof could be made the amount stated in the said Warrant, or any part thereof (or whereof could be made more than the sum of £   parcel of the amount stated in the Warrant); and serve on the said   a Copy of this Summons, and return you on the said   day of   next what you have done thereon.
    18 ,
        Clerk of the Court of the Resident Magistrate
    .   of the District of   .
[Sch. B., Sec. 48, Act No. 20, 1856.]

---

15   DECREE OR WRIT OF CIVIL IMPRISONMENT.

Court of the Resident Magistrate, District of   .
    To   , Messenger of the Court, and to the Keeper of the Public Prison of the District of   .
These are to command you, the said Messenger, to take   **of**

and deliver him to the Keeper of the Public Prison of the District aforesaid, together with this Warrant, there to be safely kept until he shall
have paid unto   of   , the sum of £   which the said
recovered for his Debt and Costs by Judgment of this Court, bearing date
the   day of   18   , or until the expiration of   months
from the day on which the said   shall be received into the said
Prison, by virtue of this Warrant, whichever of the two shall first happen,
or until the said   shall be otherwise legally discharged; and for
your so doing, this shall be your Warrant.
    Dated at   this   day of   , 18 .
    Clerk of the Court.   Resident Magistrate of the District of   .
[Sch. B., Sec. 49, Act No. 20, 1856.]

---

16   SUMMONS IN ACTION OF INTERPLEADER.
Court of the Resident Magistrate for the District of   .
    To   , Messenger of the said Court.
    Summon   of   and   of   , that they severally appear
before the Resident Magistrate of the District, to be holden at   , on
the   day of   , 18   , at   o'clock in the Forenoon, with
their respective Witnesses, if they have any, then to have it determined
and declared by the judgment of the said Court whether certain Movable
Property, attached on the   day of   , 18   , by you, the
said   under and by virtue of a certain Writ of Execution, issued out
of the said Court, commanding you, the said   of the Movable
Property of one   to levy and raise certain Sums of Money in the
said Writ mentioned, and which Movable Property is claimed by the
said   as being his Property, and not liable to such execution, be or
be not the Property of the said   and be or be not so liable;
and serve as well upon the said   as upon the said   a copy of
this Summons, and return you on the said   day of   , 18   ,
what you have done on this Summons.
                                        Resident Magistrate.
    Dated at   this   day of   , 18 .
    Clerk of the Court.
[Sch. B., Sec. 58, Act No. 20, 1856.]

---

17   INTERPLEADER ORDER TO PROCEED.
Court of the Resident Magistrate, District of   .
    To the Messenger of the Court.
    The Court doth order and adjudge that the Movable Property mentioned
in the Summons issued against   and   under the 58th Rule of
Court (if the Property of the said   which question the Court doth
not now decide), is, nevertheless, by Law, subject to attachment and
execution under the Warrant or Writ issued in the case of   against
       the said Warrant or Writ being issued for the recovery of the rent
due and owing for the occupation of the premises in which the said
Movable Property was, with the consent of the said   placed and
kept, in such a manner as to be liable for such rent, and that the further
execution of the said Writ or Warrant be proceeded with in like manner
as if no claim thereto had been made by the said   . You are,
therefore, hereby authorized and required to proceed accordingly.
    These are also to require you that of the Movable Property of the
said   you cause to be levied the sum of £   for costs in favour
of the said   adjudged by the Court against the said   together
with your charges (if any) about the same, for which this shall be your
Warrant.
    Given under my hand, at   this   day of   , 18 .
    Clerk of the Court.   Resident Magistrate.
[Act No. 20, of 1856, Rule LVIII.]

18 ORDER TO DELIVER UP GOODS ATTACHED.

Court of the Resident Magistrate, District of .

To the Messenger of the Court.

The Court doth order and adjudge that the Movable Property mentioned in the Summons issued against   and   under the 58th Rule of Court, is the Property of the said   and that the further execution of the Warrant or Writ issued in the case of   against   be stayed as against the said Movable Property, and that the said Movable Property be delivered by you to the said .

These are also to require you that of the Movable Property of the said   you cause to be levied the sum of £   for costs in favour of the said   adjudged by the Court against the said   together with your charges (if any) about the same, for which this shall be your Warrant.

Given under my hand, at   this   day of   , 18 .
Resident Magistrate.

Clerk of the Court.

[Act No. 20, of 1856, Rule LVIII.]

---

19 INTERPLEADER ORDER TO PROCEED.

Court of the Resident Magistrate, District of .

To the Messenger of the Court.

The Court doth order and adjudge that the Movable Property mentioned in the Summons issued against   and   under the 58th Rule of Court, is not the Property of the said   and is liable to be sold in execution under and by virtue of Warrant or Writ issued in the case of   against   for the recovery of the moneys in the said Writ mentioned. You are, therefore, hereby authorized and required to proceed as directed by the aforesaid Writ or Warrant.

These are also to require you that of the Movable Property of the said   you cause to be levied the sum of £   for costs in favour of the said   adjudged by the Court against the said   together with your charges (if any) about the same, for which this shall be your Warrant.

Given under my hand, at   this   day of   , 18 .
Resident Magistrate.

Clerk of the Court.

[Act No. 20, of 1856, Rule LVIII.]

---

20 SUMMONS IN ACTION OF EJECTMENT.

Court of the Resident Magistrate, District of .

To   Messenger of the said Court.

Summon   of   , that he appear before the Court of the Resident Magistrate of this District, to be holden at   on the   day of   next, at   o'clock in the Forenoon, to show why he shall not be condemned to yield and deliver up to   of   , possession of a certain   situated at   held by the said   from and under the said   for the amount of certain Rent or Hire, due and in arrear from the said   to the said   in regard to the said   amounting, together with the Costs, to the sum of £   for which a Warrant of Execution was, on the   day of   last, duly sued out under a Judgment of this Court, against the Movable Property of the said   on which Warrant a return has been duly made, that no such Movable Property as aforesaid has been found whereof could be made the Amount stated in the said Warrant, or any part thereof; and serve upon the said   a Copy of this Summons, and return you on the said   day of   18 , what you have done thereon.

Dated at   this   day of   , 18 .

Clerk to the Court of the Resident Magistrate of   .

[Sch. B., Sec. 50, Act No. 20, 1856.]

21

Court of the Resident Magistrate, District of
To   Messenger of the said Court.
It having appeared to this Court that   of   holds from and
under   of   a certain   and that the said   who has recovered Judgment and sued out Execution against the Movable Property
of the said   for the Amount of certain rent of the said   due and
in arrear, hath not had of the said Movable Property, or otherwise, the
Amount of the said Rent, or any part thereof; and the said   having
afterwards, to wit, on   day of   18 , by the Judgment of this
Court, been duly decreed to be put into possession of the said
This is, therefore, to authorize and require you to put the said
into possession of the same by removing therefrom the said   and all
other persons claiming from, through, or under him, for which this shall
be your Warrant; and return you on the   day of   18 , what
you have done in pursuance thereof.
Given under my hand at   this   day of   18 .
Clerk of the Court.   Resident Magistrate for the District of
[Sch. B., Sec. 51, Act No. 20, 1856.]

22

of   , maketh oath and saith that   of   , is justly
and truly indebted to this Deponent in the sum of £   for the Arrears
of a certain   Rent, due and payable by the said   to the said
Deponent, for the Hire and Occupation, from and under this Deponent of
a certain   situated at   which said sum of £   has been
demanded from the said   for the space of seven days and upwards,
reckoned from this day, but has not yet been paid.
Sworn before me this   day of   18 , at
Resident Magistrate for the District of
[Sch. B, Sec. 52, Act No. 20, 1856.]

23

Whereas   of   , hath this day made oath before me that
of   , holds from and under him, as Tenant or Occupant, a certain
and that there is now justly due and owing by the said   to the
said   the sum of £   for   Month's Rent of the said   and
whereas the said   hath applied to me for an Order for the Seizure
and Arrest of Movable Property, according to the provisions of the Act in
that behalf made and provided; and whereas   of   , hath agreed
to join the said   in giving the Security in the said Section mentioned :
Now, therefore, the said   and the said   do hereby, jointly
and severally promise and undertake, to and with the said Resident
Magistrate, and his Assigns, that the said   shall, not later than the
        day of   unless the Rent due and in arrear as aforesaid shall be
sooner paid and satisfied, or unless the said   shall sooner consent
under the provisions of the Act aforesaid, to a Sale, without Suit, of the
Movable Property which may be seized and arrested by virtue of the said
Order, "sue out from the Court of the said Resident Magistrate, a
Summons against the said   for the recovery of the Rent or Hire
aforesaid, and shall prosecute the same to Judgment, without any unnecessary delay," and that the said   and   or either of them, at
the option of the said Resident Magistrate or his Assigns, shall pay, satisfy,
and make good, to or for the use of the said   or whom else it may
concern, all Damage, Costs, and Charges which he or they may receive or
sustain by reason of or in connection with, the execution of the Order

aforesaid, in case the said   shall fail to prove in the Suit or Action
aforesaid, that the said amount of Rent to be therein demanded is due and
in arrear.
Dated at   , this   day of   18 .
Before me,   Resident Magistrate.
[Sch. B. Sect. 53, Act No. 20, 1856.]

24   DISTRAINT FOR RENT.

To   , Messenger of the Court of the Resident Magistrate for the
    District of   .
    This is to authorize and require you to repair, as by Law provided, to
the Dwelling   situate at   and there demand Payment of the
Sum of £   ; being the Amount of certain Rent or Hire of the said
        due by   to   of   ; and in case such Payment shall
not be made then require that so much Movable Property may be pointed
out, by Law distrainable for the Rent so in arrear, as you shall deem
sufficient to satisfy the said Sum of £   , and make an Inventory of
such Property, and lay an Attachment thereon, under the provisions of
the Act in that behalf made and provided; but if no such Property shall
be pointed out, then seize and arrest, according to the provisions of the
said Act, so much of such Property as you shall deem sufficient; and
further act in that behalf as by the said Act directed; and return, on the
        day of   18 , what you shall have done under this order.
    Given under my hand at   this   day of   18 .
        Resident Magistrate for the District of
[Sch. B., Sect. 54, Act No. 20, 1856.]

25   ORDER FOR SALE OF GOODS.

To   Messenger of the Court of the Resident Magistrate for the
    District of
    Whereas you did, on the   day of   18 , in pursuance of an
Order to that effect by me issued, seize and arrest, in security for Rent
due and in arrear, certain Movable Property, then being in and upon
certain Premises, to wit, a   situated at   held and occupied by
        from and under   and whereas the said   hath appeared
before me, and hath, in order to save the expense of   an Action for
the recovery of the said Rent, admitted that he owes the same, amounting
to the Sum of £   , and hath also consented that the said Movable
Property now under Attachment should be sold, in satisfaction, or part
satisfaction, of the said Sum;
    Now, therefore, these are to authorize and require you to sell, in manner
and form as by the 32nd Section of the Act No.   , of 1855, prescribed
on the   day of   18 , at   the said Movable Property, so
attached as aforesaid, or so much thereof as may be necessary for the
purpose of making of the proceeds the said Sum of £   so due and
owing to the said   and your legal Charge for holding the said Sale;
and pay to the said   the said Sum, and retain your said Charges, and
return to me, in the Court of the Resident Magistrate of the District, on
the   day of   18 , what you shall have done in pursuance
hereof.
    Given under my hand, this   day of   18 , at
        Resident Magistrate of
[Sec. B, Sec. 57, Act No. 20, 1856.]

26   NOTICE OF INVENTORY AND SEIZURE.

    Take Notice, that I have this day seized and arrested the Articles com-
prised in the above Inventory, in pursuance of an Order to me directed,
under the hand of   Esq., Resident Magistrate for the District of

whereby I am authorized and required to seize and arrest Movable Property distrainable for Rent, sufficient to satisfy to   the sum of £   due to him by you for Rent in arrear, as well as my legal Charges about the said Order.
Dated this   day of   18 , at
Messenger of the Court of the Resident Magistrate for the District of
[Sch. B, Sec. 55, Act No. 20, 1856.]

---

27   BOND—SECURITY FOR MOVABLES ATTACHED.
Court of the Resident Magistrate, District of
        To   Messenger of the said Court.
Whereas   Messenger of the Court of Resident Magistrate for the District of   by virtue of an Order under the hand of   Esq.,
Resident Magistrate of the said District, bearing date the   day of
   18   has seized and arrested, in Security for the Sum of
being the amount of certain Rent, due in arrear from   of   to
of   the undermentioned Articles, to wit:
Now, therefore, the said   and   of   do hereby jointly and severally promise and undertake, to and with the said   that the said Movable Property shall not be made away with or disposed of, but that the same shall remain in possession of the said   under the effect of the said arrest, to abide the event of a Suit to be brought in the Court of the Resident Magistrate aforesaid, by the said   against the said   for the recovery of the said Rent or Sum of £   otherwise the said   hereby undertakes and binds himself to pay and satisfy to the said   the amount of any such Judgment which he may recover against the said   for the said Rent or Sum of £   together with his Costs of Suit.
In Witness whereof, the said   and the said   have hereunto set their hands this   day of   18 .
[Sch. B, Sec. 56, Act No. 20, 1856.]

---

28   NOTICE TO QUIT.
Court of the Resident Magistrate for
        Messenger of the Court.
Summon   of   that he forthwith quit and deliver up to of   the occupation of a certain House, Garden, and Premises, the property of the said   and if he shall fail to do so, then summon the said   of   that he appear before the Court of the Resident Magistrate of   to be holden at   , on the   day of   at
   o'clock in the Forenoon, with his Witnesses (if he have any), and show cause why he hath not done so.—and serve on the said   a copy of this Summons,   and return you on that Day to the said Court what you have done in this Summons.
Clerk of the Court.

---

29   WRIT OF EJECTMENT.
Court of the Resident Magistrate for the District of
        Messenger of the Court.
Whereas, in a certain Case in the Court before me, wherein   of   was the Plaintiff, and   of   was the Defendant, the said   on the   day of   obtained the Judgment of the said Court against the said   , decreeing and ordaining him, the said   , to remove himself, his Family, Servants, Goods, and whole concerns, from and out of all occupation and possession whatever, of a certain Dwelling-house, Garden, and Premises, belonging to the said   , as at present

occupied by the said   , on the   day of   , and to leave the
same open, to the end that the said   may peaceably enter thereto and
possess the same :—This is, therefore, to require you that you cause the
said   to remove himself, his Family, Servants, Goods, and whole
concerns, from and out of all occupation and possession whatever of the
said Dwelling-house, Garden, and Premises, on the   day of   ,
and to leave the same open, to the end that the said   may peaceably
enter thereto and possess the same :—And, also, that of the Goods and
Chattels of the said   you cause to be levied and raised the sum of
          which the said   recovered by the Judgment of the said Court
against the said   for the Costs and Charges of the said   by him
about his Suit on that behalf expended, whereof the said   was also
convicted, together with your Charges about the same, and pay to the said
Plaintiff the Costs aforesaid ; — and return to the Clerk of this Court
what you have done by virtue hereof, for which this shall be your
Warrant.

Given under my hand, at   , this   day of   , 18 .
Clerk of the Court.

LONDON : PRINTED BY WILLIAM CLOWES AND SONS, LIMITED,
STAMFORD STREET AND CHARING CROSS.

www.ingramcontent.com/pod-product-compliance
Lightning Source LLC
Chambersburg PA
CBHW030625270326
41927CB00007B/1312